BRI...

GARDEN *KNOW-HOW*

BRIGHT AND EASY BORDERS

How to plan, plant and maintain beautiful borders, with step-by-step photographs

BARBARA SEGALL

southwater

This edition is published by Southwater

Southwater is an imprint of Anness Publishing Ltd
Hermes House, 88–89 Blackfriars Road, London SE1 8HA
tel. 020 7401 2077; fax 020 7633 9499
www.southwaterbooks.com; info@anness.com

UK agent: The Manning Partnership Ltd,
6 The Old Dairy, Melcombe Road, Bath BA2 3LR;
tel. 01225 478444; fax 01225 478440; sales@manning-partnership.co.uk

UK distributor: Grantham Book Services Ltd,
Isaac Newton Way, Alma Park Industrial Estate, Grantham, Lincs NG31 9SD;
tel. 01476 541080; fax 01476 541061; orders@gbs.tbs-ltd.co.uk

North American agent/distributor: National Book Network,
4501 Forbes Boulevard, Suite 200, Lanham, MD 20706;
tel. 301 459 3366; fax 301 429 5746; www.nbnbooks.com

Australian agent/distributor: Pan Macmillan Australia,
Level 18, St Martins Tower, 31 Market St, Sydney, NSW 2000;
tel. 1300 135 113; fax 1300 135 103; customer.service@macmillan.com.au

New Zealand agent/distributor: David Bateman Ltd,
30 Tarndale Grove, Off Bush Road, Albany, Auckland;
tel. (09) 415 7664; fax (09) 415 8892

A CIP catalogue record for this book is available from the British Library.

Publisher: Joanna Lorenz
Editorial Manager: Helen Sudell
Designer: Alan Marshall
Photography credits listed on page 96
Illustrations: Michael Shoebridge

Previously published as *Step-by-Step Beautiful Borders*

1 3 5 7 9 10 8 6 4 2

CONTENTS

INTRODUCTION

The border is a traditional garden feature, a place where we can grow our choice and favourite plants to show them off to best advantage. In ground that has been well-prepared they can be maintained easily and enjoyed for their special ornamental qualities. All plants have their individual attractions, but in a border it is the way in which they become an entity that is so interesting. How they combine, how their foliage and flowers mingle, and the definition that different shapes give, are the factors that make a border so pleasing to look at.

At the simplest level, I define a border as an area set aside specially for the cultivation of the plants we have come to appreciate as traditional border plants, including hardy perennials, half-hardy annuals, bulbs, shrubs, grasses and decorative herbs. But beyond this explanation, at another level, the border is the expression of creative and artistic talents of individual garden owners.

The borders in this book have been chosen primarily for their beauty, but they are also examples of how specific aspects of the site, soil conditions, seasons, colour combinations and even the shape of the border, can all play a part in making wonderful garden effects. There are also borders that rely on special groups of plants for their style and beauty. These include grass borders, edible borders, herb and rose borders, as well as single genus borders filled with many examples of one particular group of plants, and borders whose beauty lies in their foliage rather than their flowers. Each border is illustrated with photographs that show it at its best, as well as a sketch plan for the planting.

For the experienced border-maker, as well as the first-time border-creator, I hope that the gardens in this book will inspire even greater border designs, and offer plenty of new ideas.

Designs for borders

A well-designed border brings out the most interesting and individual combinations of plants – garden visits, photographs and sketches are the means to develop ideas, translating someone else's garden schemes into your own setting. This is an acceptable form of copying, and most gardeners, generous and open about their planting ideas, are quick to acknowledge the source of their inspirations.

PLANNING A BORDER

The main elements you should be aware of in the design and planning of a beautiful border are: season, site, soil, colour scheme and form or shape of the border. There are also the plant themes to consider, such as roses, foliage or giant plants; or where you use the plants to create a subtle effect, as in a romantic or meditative border.

SEASON

Most borders have times when there is not a full display of colour and foliage, but if you are able to plan well, it is possible to have some interest in the border at most times of the year.

In spring, bulbs and early flowering plants such as primula, pulmonaria and wallflowers provide bright splashes of colour to cheer the gardener's heart after winter. But by late spring and early summer the rush to grow and flower, or produce attractive foliage, is well under way. In late summer and autumn, colour and form come from bright and hot colours, and as the season turns into winter, seedheads, grass panicles and evergreens or evergreys offer a continuity of interest.

SHAPES

The shape of the border will determine the style and look of your planting scheme. A formal border, where the plants are repeated in a definite pattern, is one of the breathtaking wonders of gardening. It looks good in a large garden, but can be equally attractive in a small garden, if the setting invites such formality.

Left: *This narrow border is only about 1.2m (4ft) wide, but herbaceous perennials have been allowed to tumble over at the front to provide useful colour contrasts with the yellow shrub behind. This is the evergreen* Choisya ternata *'Sundance' with* Aster novi-belgii *'Audrey' (left) and 'Jenny' (right) and a pink chrysanthemum in the centre. In front is a pink-flowered rock rose that would have bloomed in late spring and early summer. This kind of combination of shrubs and herbaceous plants ensures season-long colour.*

Formal borders are straight-edged and backed by evergreen hedges, which act as frames or backdrops for the border's palette of plant colours. Such a border can really only be viewed from the front, unless there are formal paths leading up to it, at right-angles to the grass and to the hedges.

Borders do not have to have straight edges, however, although it can be a plus when it comes to mowing the lawn around the border. One of the most innovative borders featured in this book is a double circular border, which has many different looks to it, depending on where you are standing and whether you are looking at it inwards or outwards.

Less formal than a long, traditional straight border, but equally creative, is an island bed which can be seen from all round, so every part of it has to have an attractive look. Island beds usually have one or several high points that take the eye from ground level plants at the edges of the border to the middle. It is not necessary to have a formal, repeated pattern, unless the style calls for a rigid bedding-type planting.

Moving the eye upwards is a part of the design of any area of the garden, and this can be fully achieved where a border backs onto a wall or fence, and a vertical border can be created.

Right: *This very narrow bed shows how charmingly shrubs and herbaceous plants may be combined. However, if slugs are a problem in your garden, you may find the hostas are an unwise choice.*

The plants

The position of a border will have a bearing on the type of plants you can use in it. If it is in sun or shade, or in a damp or dry soil, limits on your planting will be imposed. The range to choose from is wide, however, and only a small percentage will find their way into most gardens. Roses, grasses, foliage plants, annuals, perennials, half-hardy plants, shrubs, small trees, climbing plants, herbs, bulbs and even vegetables are on the list of plants that bring borders to life.

Above: *A traditional herbaceous border at the peak of its summer glory, this richly planted section is an inspiration to us all.*

CHOOSING A COMBINATION

In the herbaceous borders shown in this book, the richness of colour and shape, height and depth is impressive. Mixing herbaceous plants and shrubs is an extension of the herbaceous border, and has long been an approach to combining a wide range of plants with differing heights, spreads and ornamental attractions. Single genus borders showing their variety of colour and form to best advantage, can be equally successful.

The plants available for use in the border provide many ornamental attractions, and these need not be their flowers alone. Foliage is on the plant for much longer than the flowers in many cases, and it offers colour – green, grey, grey-blue, golden, purple, silver and creamy-green variegations – as well as texture. Feathery ferns, stately parasol-shaped foliage of *Darmera peltata*, metallic rodgersia and spiky iris foliage all look dramatic in a border display.

Some plants, such as *Verbena bonariensis* and *Gaura lindheimeri*, carry their delicate flowers on long stems high above the main plant mound. These plants are useful as "see-through" plants. They cover the ground, but they do not make a dense mass and their flowers peep out from other plant foliage, offering a double effect.

FRAGRANCE

Fragrance also attributes to a border's success. It acts like a magnet, drawing you towards it as you try to find the flowers from which it comes. By placing scented plants or those with aromatic foliage strategically, you can encourage your visitors to move on to each new delight.

COLOUR

As for colour, the green of foliage is usually the main background colour. It provides the foil for some stunning colour combinations, especially in late summer borders where fiery reds and sunny yellows are used. Such hot colours are show-stoppers in their season, but make for a restless effect, so it is best to use them sparingly and just for special effects, when their energetic and invigorating display can be enjoyed. Soft pastels, with silvery and purple foliage plants, create a quiet and tranquil scene and because they tend to draw you in, can make a garden or border seem larger and more flowing.

Using just one or two colours as the dominant motif in a plant scheme can be a very effective way of uniting a group of plants. As you walk along or around the border, you will involuntarily find that you are looking for the next patch of whatever the chosen colour is. The colour scheme is leading you through the garden.

PUTTING IT ALL TOGETHER

Combining border plants is an individual choice, but there are one or two basic rules that make for successful and attractive associations. Plants are living, growing things and so, as the season moves on, they change. You have to envisage what they will look like as they grow, and imagine them moving from spring foliage to summer flowers in sequence. To hold this ephemeral, moving picture together you need to give the border some strong structural and focal elements. Evergreen shrubs, a strong green hedge as a backdrop or plants with spiky or architectural foliage or stature, are the main ways to supply this semi-permanent structure to the border. You can provide focal points with a variety of statues, wall fountains, benches or chimney pots.

It is obvious that low-growing plants are more easily seen if placed at the front of a border, and it is usual to grade the heights of planting by setting the intermediate and taller plants to the back. However, you can bend the rules and plant taller ones near the front – the screening effect can be exciting. When the taller plants such as opium poppies, which have attractive grey foliage at first, have reached full height and are flowering, a delicate focus is provided, offering greater depth to the border. It can also be effective to plant some low-growing plants round the taller ones near the back of the border. As you look closely into the border, your eyes are tugged by pools of colour from one part to another.

You do not have to use ground level as the starting point for your border ambitions. Instead, grow climbing plants up a wall, or a wall-fixed trellis. This will then form a backdrop to a border. Roses, clematis, honeysuckle, pyracantha and climbers, including golden hop and the climbing nasturtium, *Tropaeolum peregrinum,* are among the plants that can be used to take the border interest upwards.

PLANNING THE BORDER
When you begin, make a list of the plants you would like to have in the border, noting their height, spread and flowering times. Play around with a

sketchpad and work out where they should be planted in the border. At first, especially when starting with small plants, the border will look quite bare, but once the plant roots get established and the growing season is under way, they will spread quickly to cover the ground. To get a less rigid effect, plant in uneven numbers.

Always keep a note of the plants, and as the border develops over the year, note those that perform well, too well or not at all, as well as your own planting mismatches. Then, in the autumn you can remedy the situation by replacing the non-doers and re-organizing any unharmonious combinations.

BORDERS IN CONTAINERS
Even if you have no garden to speak of, you can still grow an attractive border, but instead of growing it in the ground, you have to use all manner of containers to hold it. On gravel, hard-standing patios and balconies you can grow an effective border by choosing the plants that offer the same ornament as border plants and moving them round until you find the combination that pleases you most. Unlike plants grown in a border in a fixed position, the container border is a truly mobile concept and can be mixed and matched whenever you bring home a new plant. When any plant does not perform well or dies, it can be easily replaced.

Choose plants that have a long flowering period, are evergreen, or look good in more than one season, with flowers, hips and good foliage colour, for example. Many grasses and conifers do well in containers.

PLANTING A CLIMBER

1 Make sure that the support is in place first, then dig a hole large enough to take the root ball comfortably. The plant should be about 45cm (18in) away from the wall, where the soil is less dry. Fork over the base of the hole, and work in plenty of garden compost or well-rotted manure.

2 Position the plant so that it leans towards the wall at 45 degrees, and use a cane or stick to check that the root ball is level with the surrounding soil.

3 Tease out a few roots from the root ball, then return the soil. Firm in well to ensure that there are no large air pockets. Water thoroughly.

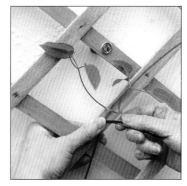

4 If the stems are secured to a cane or support in the pot, untie them and train the shoots to the wall support. Spread them out widely, taking them horizontally as well as vertically, so that the base of the plant will not be bare.

Making borders

In general, try to match the size of your border to the amount of time and energy you can devote to it. At the same time, however, you should try to make its physical proportions match those of the house and the garden as a whole.

MOWING EDGE

1 Lay the paving slabs on the grass for positioning, and use a half-moon edger to cut a new edge.

2 Slice off the grass with a spade, and remove enough soil for a couple of centimetres of sand and gravel mix, mortar and the slabs. Consolidate the sub-base.

3 Use five blobs of mortar on which to bed the slab, and then tap the paving level using a mallet or the handle of a club hammer.

4 Make sure the slabs are flush with the lawn, and use a spirit level to check that the slabs are laid evenly. Mortar the joints for a neat finish, otherwise weeds will grow in them.

MAKING A BORDER IN A LAWN

A linear shape, rectangular or square, with straight edges is the traditional choice for a formal border. Such a border is usually edged with brick or paving to make an edge for the mower and reduce the maintenance in the garden. The plants in the border can flow over its edge onto the brick or paving and will not be damaged by, nor in the way of, the mower. A formal straight-edged border should be of substantial width, so that it makes an impact with the planting you choose. If the border is narrow, it will not have the depth for several changes of height, nor for the pools of colour that make such borders so attractive to look at.

To begin with, you will have to lift the turf. Mark out the shape of the border using pegs and string lines if it is to be linear in shape. If it is to be curved or circular, use a piece of hosing to mark it out, within a linear framework. This makes it easier to remove the turf. Then you can put the turf back at the edges of the circle.

Using a semi-circular bladed edging tool, cut out several rows of turf to make it easier to lift them. To lift away each turf, use a sharp-edged spade or a turfing spade to slide under the turf surface. As far as possible, avoid treading on the newly-opened soil surface, or you will compact it more than it already is.

When you have lifted sufficient turf, you will need to aerate the soil. Double dig it, fork it over and then add well-rotted manure or compost to it to give it a good texture and to give the plants a good start. Whatever type of soil predominates in your garden,

for the best results in terms of plant growth, it needs to be open and have a good texture so that the roots can get well down into it and become established. Double digging to a depth of 45-60cm (18-24in) should do this. The soil should also be well drained. If necessary, you may need to dig in drainage channels, or add grit or sand to the soil when you double dig, to improve drainage.

After double digging, leave the soil to settle over the autumn, and in winter the action of frost and rain will make the soil more friable and crumbly. A traditional term for this is hazelling: the soil wrinkles and crumbles, looking like the rough brown skin of a hazel nut. The action of earthworms and other soil organisms also helps to improve the soil's condition.

As they grow, plants will need nutrients throughout a long growing period and this should be dug in as compost or manure when you prepare new ground. Or you can add it to the border in spring as a compost mulch. Mulching will also help to protect the soil surface, preventing it from drying out in periods of drought, and once the compost mulch is dragged down into the soil, it will offer nutrients in the soil to the plant.

An attractive edging of brick.

RENOVATING A PREVIOUSLY CULTIVATED BORDER

When renovating a previously cultivated border, you have to improve the soil condition. Dig out all perennial weeds such as bindweed, ground elder, marestail and couch grass. These are invasive weeds that will take some work to get rid of, since any part that breaks off can become a weed plant in its own right. The best time to remove such weeds is in the spring when their growth is fresh and the soil friable enough to dig over. You can also weaken them by laying black plastic across the site for a few weeks, so depriving them of light. Before you start on the border, lift the plastic and dig out the feeble strands on the weeds.

Perennial weeds with long tap roots, such as dock, should be levered out with a fork. It is easy to remove them when they are young in the spring and when the ground is moist just after a spring shower. To prevent a huge crop of them from year to year, remove the flowerheads and seeds of any that get away before you dig them out.

You will also need to remove stones and other debris. If there are any existing plants that you want to save, dig them out and heel them into a holding bay in another part of the garden until you are ready to add them to the new planting.

MAKING A GRAVEL BORDER

Gravel beds provide an attractive site and considerably reduce the maintenance in terms of weeds. A gravel bed also offers the perfect site for plants such as grasses, lavender, yucca and many alpines that prefer well-drained, dry conditions.

A gravel border is normally used for a small collection of plants and makes a change of pace between intensive flower and foliage planted borders. Gravel can also be used in place of lawn and paths, giving the impression of a dry river bed, with the border plants as islands of colour. It is a perfect surface for plants to self-seed into, and it is easy to take any that are too abundant and replant them elsewhere. When you begin to plant the border, use a fork or a trowel to remove the layer of gravel, make slits in the membrane and dig a planting hole.

GRAVEL BEDS

1 Mark out the bed with rope, a hose or by sprinkling sand where you think the outline should be. Check you are happy with its position and size. Then cut the outline of the bed using a half-moon edger. A spade will do, but this does not produce such a crisp edge.

2 Lift the grass within the bed with a spade, removing about 10cm (4in) from the surface. The finished bed must be a couple of inches below the grass, otherwise the gravel will spill onto the lawn and damage the mower.

3 Spread a generous quantity of garden compost or rotted manure over the surface, and add a slow- or controlled-release fertilizer. Then fork this in to loosen and enrich the soil. If the ground is poorly drained and you want to grow dry soil plants, work in plenty of coarse grit too. This is an important stage as it is difficult to improve the soil once the gravel is in place.

Above: *A gravelled area. Gravel beds can be heavily planted with a combination of drought-resistant plants. The weed-suppressing gravel will mean they mainly look after themselves.*

4 Spread about 5cm (2in) of gravel over the soil, making sure it is kept off the lawn and will not spill onto it.

The soil in your garden

The soil is probably the most important element of your borders – the plants depend on it for water and nutrition. Get the soil right at the beginning and you will have a wonderful collection of plants in your borders.

THE TYPE OF SOIL
The soil you have in your garden is the most precious basic material for beautiful borders, so you have to take care of it. Never attempt to work it when the weather is very dry or very wet, or when the soil is covered in frost or snow. In these kinds of conditions, any pressure on the soil will compact it, or in the case of dry conditions, erode it. In frost and snow, it will simply be too hard to shift at all. Border soil is traditionally prepared in the autumn or springtime, when it is easier and far more pleasant to work with.

HOW GOOD IS YOUR SOIL?
The basic ingredient of any planting scheme is the soil. The best results are achieved by paying attention to getting the growing site in as good a condition as possible, before you even purchase or propagate a plant. Remember that once you have plants in the soil, it will be difficult to get at it again to dig it over or add compost in bulk. You will, of course, be able to add mulches and compost in selected areas, but never to the whole border, unless you renovate it completely.

TESTING FOR MAJOR NUTRIENTS
Plants need nutrients to be available to them, and these are held in solution in the soil and absorbed by the roots. They are used with carbon dioxide and water to make food for the plants. Phosphorus, potassium, magnesium, calcium and sulphur are needed in fairly large quantities for plants to thrive. Trace elements including manganese and chlorine are also needed in smaller quantities.

You can test the soil for major nutrients – nitrogen (keeps the plant growing well), phosphorus in the form of phosphates (encourages root growth) and potassium (gives greater impetus to flowers and fruiting) need to be applied regularly.

1 Gather your soil sample, using a trowel, from 5-8cm (2-3in) below the surface. Take several samples from around the garden, and test each one separately.

2 Mix 1 part soil to 5 parts water. Shake or stir the mixture in a clean jar, then allow it to settle – it may take half an hour to a day to become reasonably clear (clay soils are the slowest).

3 Carefully draw off some of the clear liquid from the top few centimetres for the test.

4 Using the pipette, transfer the solution to the test and reference chambers of the plastic container.

5 Pour the powder from the capsule provided into the test chamber. Replace the cap and shake vigorously until the powder has dispersed.

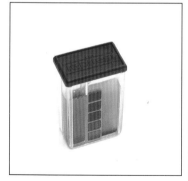

6 Wait for a few minutes for the colour to develop, then read it off against the comparison chart. There will be a key that explains the reading, and instructions to tell you how to correct any problem.

TESTING FOR STRUCTURE

For newly-cut and renovated borders, first test the type of soil you have. Begin by finding out its texture. To do this, pick up a handful of damp soil and roll it between your finger and thumb; if it feels rough and granular, but the grains don't adhere to each other, the soil is sandy. If it forms a ball when you roll it between your thumb and forefinger, it is a sandy loam. If it is rather sticky and makes a firm shape, it is a clay loam. But if you can mould it into shapes, it is a clay soil.

A clay soil presents plants with problems because the soil particles are so closely packed and moisture-retentive that the plants' delicate root hairs and root system cannot obtain water. Nor is there enough oxygen available in the soil for them to use. In effect, the root system cannot move and so becomes trapped in a waterlogged soil. During the summer, a clay soil bakes hard and dry, and great fissures or cracks appear all over the surface. To improve a clay soil, either put in a drainage channel or add grit and sand to the soil when you prepare it for planting. Adding compost or manure will also help, as both these improve the structure of the soil and aerate it.

ACID OR ALKALINE

You can determine whether a soil is acid or alkaline by measuring the soil pH. This is done on a scale which ranges from 1 to 14, and can be tested with small samples of garden soil. Take some samples from your garden and use a soil tester kit to see what the pH level of your soil is. If the reading is below 7, then the soil is acid or sour. If it is at 7, the soil is neutral and if it is above 7, it is alkaline. The pH level is determined by the amount of calcium there is in the soil – this is an element necessary to many plants that is usually washed out of the soil by the action of water. It can be boosted if you lime the soil, and then you can increase the range of plants you can have in the border.

On an acid soil where the pH is below 7, you will be able to grow fewer plants, and only those that tolerate acid conditions, such as azaleas and rhododendrons. Also, fewer plants will tolerate a soil with a high pH level (very alkaline), as vital minerals will be missing.

The best type of soil for healthy, all-round growth of a good range of plants is a loam soil with an average pH content between 5.5 and 7.5. In this type of soil there will be good drainage and the necessary water retention, as well as high fertility. Soil organisms that help to aerate the soil and break down bulky organic matter are also more prevalent in a soil with an average pH level.

FERTILIZING THE SOIL

Where a number of plants are growing and competing for space, light, water and nutrients, you will need to fertilize most soils if you want all the plants to do equally well. Fertilizing during the growing season is particularly important. You can either do this once a week, by applying a liquid feed, or you can use slow- or controlled-release pellets or granules that hold fertilizer. If you apply fertilizer in the form of concentrated mixes of blood, fish and bone, apply them during warm weather in the spring, when the activity of soil organisms helps in their slow release into the soil.

Of the inorganic chemical fertilizers, soluble ones are easier to handle, give value for money, and they act as they are applied, but they have to be used regularly during the growing season. They can also be washed away or leached out of quick-draining soils. Slow-release fertilizers are expensive, but they are not washed away or leached out of the soil, and need only be applied once during the growing season.

FEEDING BORDERS

1 Most established plants, but especially demanding ones such as roses, benefit from annual feeding. Apply a slow- or controlled-release fertilizer in spring or early summer, sprinkling it around the bushes. Keep it away from the stem, sprinkling it further out where most of the active root growth is.

2 Hoe it into the surface so that it penetrates the root area more quickly.

3 Unless rain is expected, water it in. This will make the fertilizer active more quickly in dry conditions.

PLANTS FOR ACID SOIL
If your soil is acid, without altering its nature you can still enjoy a range of plants including camellias, heathers, rhododendrons, azaleas, pieris, witch hazel and the strawberry tree.

PLANTS FOR ALKALINE SOIL
Many shrubs and perennials will grow well in an alkaline soil, so the range and choice here is greater. Anchusa, bergenia, galega, hellebore, heuchera, kniphofia, peony, verbascum and brunnera are among the perennials; box, hebe, buddleja, choisya, philadelphus and Jerusalem sage are among those shrubs which will grow particularly well in such a soil.

Planting up the border

After you have tested the soil and determined the soil type and the acid or alkaline character of it, you can decide which plants will do best in it. Although you can alter the nature of the soil, it is probably easier to opt for the plants that are known to do well in the conditions you have.

WHEN TO PLANT

Traditionally, spring and autumn are considered the best times for planting, when the soil is either just warming up or still warm enough for the plants to get established. This was also the only time that field-grown plants were available to gardeners. Now with so many herbaceous plants and shrubs available as container-grown plants, the advice to plant in these two seasons is not always necessary. Provided the soil is workable, i.e. it is not frosty, waterlogged or too dry, you can plant up at any time of the year.

Before planting, water the plants in their containers. If you are planting up a large border, set the plants out into the positions you have chosen for them, section by section, and get an idea of how they will look. Dig planting holes large enough to take the roots comfortably and deep enough to keep the plants at the same level to which they were planted in the containers. Backfill the planting holes with the soil you have taken out. Water the plants well, swirling water and soil into the planting holes. Then firm the surface down and water regularly until the plants are well established.

TYPES OF BORDER

The main principles to remember when designing a border are that it is a place to grow choice plants well and in harmonious combination with each other. You can create tranquil moods with pastel colours, or fire the imagination with brightly-coloured flowers and angular foliage.

The bones, or structure, of the border will come from evergreen and shapely deciduous shrubs. They will provide a mass and greater interest, especially if their foliage has autumn colours. The border's ultimate form then comes from the shapes of plants. Some, low-growing and small plants with delicate flowers, will

PLANTING A BORDER

1 Always make sure the pots have been watered before planting, otherwise the root ball may remain dry as water runs off it when watering after planting.

2 Space the plants in their pots before you start to plant, as changes are easy at this stage. Try to visualize the plants at their final height and spread, and don't be tempted to plant them too close.

3 Knock the plant out of its pot only when you are ready to plant, so that the roots are not exposed unnecessarily to the drying air. Carefully tease out some of the roots.

4 Plant small plants with a trowel, large ones with a spade, and always work methodically from the back or from one end of the border.

5 Return the soil and make sure the plant is at its original depth or just a little deeper. Firm it with your hands or a heel to expel large pockets of air in the soil.

6 Water thoroughly unless the weather is wet. Be prepared to water regularly in dry weather for at least the first few weeks after planting.

need close inspection, while others, growing taller and flowering at a greater height, will rise out of the border and appear to float in bands of colour above it. Each plant association should work well as an individual combination, and as a whole in the rest of the border. Look at the border as a series of small cameos and as a whole sweep of interesting plant and colour combinations.

BORDER COLOURS

The colours of flowers, foliage, berries and stems are perhaps the most evocative of all elements in the border. Using pale pastel colours you can create a quiet, serene effect, whereas hot vibrant colours in late summer make the opposite statement and are challenging to create. You can also make an interesting display using a restricted colour palette, or even just one colour. It is fun to find the plants in such a scheme that will provide you with a succession of blooms or foliage through many seasons.

If your garden is small or non-existent under the paving of a patio or balcony, do not despair: you can still grow a border by creating a mobile garden in containers. Although it will need higher maintenance than one grown directly into the soil, since you will have to provide water and nutrients for the plants, it can be an exciting, ever-changing scene.

If you plan well with seasonal changes in mind, you can create a succession of interest through the year to hold the cheery spring colours, strong summer colours, golden autumnal tones and fragrant blossom to take you through the winter.

PLANTING BULBS IN A BORDER

1 Excavate a hole large enough to take a group of bulbs and, if the soil is poor or impoverished, fork in garden compost or well-rotted manure.

2 Space out the bulbs, planting at a depth that will leave them covered with about twice their own depth of soil.

3 To deter slugs and encourage good drainage around the bulbs, sprinkle more grit or coarse sand around them before returning the soil.

4 If planting summer-flowering bulbs in spring, position with small canes so that you do not accidentally hoe or cultivate the area before the shoots come up.

BULBS IN THE BORDER

Much of the colour and interest in a spring border comes from flowering bulbs. Daffodils, tulips, snowdrops, bluebells, crocuses, *Iris reticulata, Cyclamen coum,* aconites, dog's tooth lilies, and hyacinths can be used "en masse" in borders or singly under trees, or – for daffodils, crocuses, bluebells and aconites – naturalized in lawns.

Plant spring-flowering bulbs, except tulips, from late August through to November so that they have a long growing season in the ground and can establish well before the cold of winter sets in. Plant tulips later, from October through to November. Plant the bulbs in layers or decks, with late-flowering varieties deeper into the ground, and early-flowering bulbs nearer

Above: *Crocuses show the true versatility of bulbs. They can be used in beds and borders to bring pockets of colour when there is not much else out, and can even be naturalized in the lawn.*

the surface. In this way, you achieve a simple succession of flowering bulbs without too much disturbance of the soil. Summer-flowering bulbs such as lilies, alliums, nerines and galtonia extend the season and continue to provide interest in early and late summer.

When bulb flowers are spent, take off the flower heads, but allow the foliage to die down

DIVIDING OVERCROWDED CLUMPS

1 If a large clump of established bulbs, such as daffodils, begins to flower poorly, overcrowding may be the cause. Lift, divide and replant. You can do this when the plants are dormant, but if you do it before the leaves die down completely it is easier to see where the clumps are.

2 Separate the clump into smaller pieces, and replant some of the large, healthy bulbs in the same place. Either discard or give away the surplus bulbs if you have too many, or replant them elsewhere.

naturally. In a border, this can make for unsightly, untidy effects, but by using raffia you can loosely tie the foliage together, but do not waste time and effort bending it over. When the foliage turns yellow, usually after about six weeks, cut it back to the ground and leave the bulbs undisturbed. If the bulbs are not hardy, such as some summer-flowering varieties, lift them and clean and dry them off before storing them for planting again next spring. Tulips should be lifted as well and stored as they are attacked by pests and disease if left in the ground during the summer.

Every two or three years it is worthwhile to lift and divide large, established clumps of bulbs. Overcrowding may reduce their flowering vigour and by dividing and replanting, you will renew their flowering capacity. You will not be able to replant all the bulbs in the same position and therefore you will need to find additional space elsewhere in the garden.

THE GARDEN AS A HABITAT

Get to know the site and soil in different parts of your garden, and plant them with the right plants for that particular habitat, as if they were outside the manipulated garden and growing where they were best suited in a natural situation. To do this well, you have to know a little about the plants you want to grow. The conditions they need are an indication of the habitats they originally came from. Epimediums, for example, with their delicate spring foliage, good autumn colour and small, but interesting flowers, suit the shadier areas of a border, a clue to their woodland edge origins.

Above: *Hostas have been planted at the front of this mixed border. The height differential gives you the benefit of two borders.*

SHRUBS IN THE BORDER

Shrubs, such as *Choisya ternata* 'Sundance', deutzia and weigela, offer bursts of foliage and flower colour that are substantial for long periods during the year, unlike some herbaceous border plants. They act as a framework, as their shapes are stronger and more pronounced, and they add height, shape, foliage and floral interest, as well as providing a variation of rhythm to the whole of the border.

ROSES IN THE BORDER

Old shrub roses, including damask, centifolia, gallica, musk, and alba, bourbon, hybrid perpetual and portland roses, make a romantic and soft addition to the border. Although they are often described as needing little attention, like most plants they respond well to care given at the right time to prevent problems later. You must remember to remove their dead or damaged wood in spring, and you should also mulch and fertilize them well in spring. If they are growing in a border where they have to compete with other plants, make sure they are well watered throughout the dry seasons. If they need spraying against black or green fly, use a beneficial insect-friendly spray, and only use it on calm windless days, when the roses are in shade. Deadhead when the blooms are spent, unless the rose is also grown for its autumn hips, in which case, leave the spent flowers in place.

Modern roses, specially bred as carpet or ground cover plants, are also highly useful in sloping borders or on banks, if you want to make a good floral effect. Often their foliage is attractive too, which extends their usefulness. They will also help to maintain the border, by suppressing weeds.

Maintaining the border

Last, but equally important, is the maintenance of the border so that it continues to please and delight its home gardener, as well as any others that may visit. Low maintenance is the aim and dream of most gardeners, but whether the garden is large or small, there will always be something to do to make the border look better. Staking, deadheading, training plants, weeding, mulching, watering – all these are part of the seasonal and regular activities that make gardening such an enjoyable pastime.

MULCHING

Once you have got all the planting done, the new border will look bare, and it will look this way for a while, until the roots are well established and the plants begin to make some top growth. To keep annual weeds down, conserve soil moisture and raise the temperature of the soil surface, it is useful to apply a mulch that acts as a ground cover. In your initial soil preparation you will have removed the bulk of the perennial weeds, but if there are any still in the soil, remove them before you apply the mulch. Do not apply a mulch in cold weather, as it will then act as an insulator of the cold conditions. Instead, mulch the soil in spring, when it has warmed up considerably. Bark chippings or compost are suitable and can be applied to a depth of 5cm (2in).

WATERING

Water in newly-planted shrubs and perennials well, continuing to do so during the first growing season. Water as much as you can during very dry seasons, but try to do this early morning or late in the day, when the plants are not in full sun, otherwise their leaves may get scorched. On really hot days, this might mean waiting until well after sunset to give the garden any real benefit from the watering.

PLANT SUPPORTS

Many perennials, including *Knautia macedonica, Gaura lindheimeri* and sisyrinchiums, will support their flower stems without any extra staking or supports that you can provide. Others though, like the sumptuous large-flowered peonies with their heavy buds and full flowers, will flop onto other plants, especially during a spring shower. At that stage it is more difficult to get into the border to put in supports or stakes to keep the peony in place. Instead, when you are planting up the border, put stakes or supports in place around the plants that are going to need it, even though it may look a bit odd until they have grown enough to warrant the support. Sweet peas, although annuals, make a lovely cottage garden effect when planted around cane wigwam supports in the centre of borders. You can use hazel twigs or pea sticks for the most natural-looking support system. Bamboo canes, metal ring stakes, as well as plastic-coated stakes also look natural, once the plants are established. All are arranged so that they either form a single support for the plant or surround it, so that the plant can grow through the support, or they form a semi-circle, simply holding it at the front so that it does not flop over other plants.

Similarly, some plants that are used as wall plants do not support themselves. Use vine eyes inserted into the masonry and linked with green plastic-coated or plain wires. Wooden trellis or plastic netting can also be used for this purpose.

WEEDING THE BORDER

Good preparation of the soil should have rid you of the deep-rooted and creeping perennial weeds, such as dock and couch grass. Once the border is planted up you will have to **remove any fresh growth carefully with a hand fork so you do not damage the border plants.** As soon as the ground

APPLYING A LOOSE MULCH

1 Prepare the ground thoroughly, digging it over and working in plenty of organic material such as rotted manure or garden compost if the soil is impoverished.

2 Loose mulches will control annual weeds and prevent new perennial ones getting a foothold. You must dig up deep-rooted perennial weeds, otherwise they could grow through the mulch.

3 Water the ground thoroughly before applying the mulch. Do not apply a mulch to dry ground. Spread the mulch thickly. The example here is bark mulch.

WEEDING

1 If annual weeds have become a problem, and you want to avoid hand weeding, some contact weedkillers can be applied. Always use a dribble bar to avoid spray drift and shield the stems and leaves of the plant with a piece of hardboard or something similar. Never use around newly-planted shrubs.

2 Some weedkillers can be used around established shrubs to prevent weed seedlings emerging. Use only around established shrubs, and in accordance with the manufacturer's instructions.

covering plants are growing well, they will begin to play their part in suppressing annual weeds which will compete with your expensive perennials and shrubs for water, light, nutrients and space. If the annual weeds persist, work carefully through the border, hoeing or hand weeding them out. Although time-consuming and sometimes awkward, hand weeding is the most effective method and, in my experience, has its therapeutic value!

In a densely planted border it is not sensible, nor is it cost-effective, to use liquid systemic chemical weedkillers. The chances of spray damage on expensive plants is high and not worth the risk. If there are perennial weeds that persist too close to the root system of the border plants, wait till autumn, and then when you are lifting and dividing large clumps, sift through the roots and remove those belonging to the weeds.

WINTER PROTECTION

Some plants that are tender or borderline hardy will need winter protection. This can either be done by mulching the soil surface above the root with straw or by setting up a temporary pole-supported hessian windbreak. As a precaution, take cuttings in autumn, so that if the plant does not survive, you will have propagated new plants to take its place. Dahlia tubers will have to be lifted, cleaned and stored in frost-free conditions. Some tender wall shrubs can be protected by making a conifer blanket of branches to keep them insulated through the winter, without digging them up and bringing them indoors.

THE TOOLS FOR THE BORDER GARDENER

For soil cultivation and preparation before planting, a **garden fork** and **garden spade** will be the main tools. They have wide heads and, in the case of forks, long and wide prongs. Once the border is planted up, it is best to use the narrow heads and prongs of a **border fork** and **spade.** These allow you to work between plants without damaging the foliage or stems of the neighbouring plants. For lifting and dividing, these narrower tools are essential.

For creating a fine tilth in preparation for seed-sowing in borders, you will need a **wide-headed garden rake**. Later, for use in the planted up border, use a narrower **border rake** to clean up fallen leaves. For weeding out of annual weeds, once the border is planted up, a **Dutch** or **Paxton hoe** is useful, and for the front, or more easily reached, areas of the border a **weeding fork** and **trowel** are the best tools. A **long-handled hand fork** is also essential for reaching into the border from the edge. A **dibber, bulb planter, edging**

blade, pruning shears and **secateurs** as well as a pair of **sharp scissors** to cut blooms for the house, are all part of the toolkit a successful border gardener needs.

Irrigation systems, with leaky hoses and intermittent sprayers, can be useful in a border and will help to reduce maintenance, but they will have to be set in place before you plant up the border, and they could work out to be quite costly. Also there may be regulations about using them, so check with your water supplier first. Otherwise a **hose** or **watering can** are your only choices to keep the border well watered.

For supporting the border there is a wide range of equipment available. **Trellis, vine eyes** and **wires** are all useful for supporting wall plants that extend the border upwards. But for herbaceous plants within the border, wigwams of **canes, plastic-covered wire hoops** for plants to grow through and, most natural of all, **hazel twigs**, are the most popular choices.

Straw layers on the soil around the crown of tender perennials will insulate them in mild winter weather, but if you live in a very cold winter area make sure that the plants you use in your border are hardy for the area.

PESTS AND DISEASES

If the soil is in good condition and fertile, the plants will be healthy and thrive unaffected by any fungal problems. However, if greenfly populations are high

and affect any roses that are in the border, you will have to spray selectively on a calm, windless day. Slugs may be a problem with young plants and seedlings but if you have animals, be careful about using slug pellets. A circle of pea shingle around vulnerable plants or crushed eggshell dropped discreetly between plants may be all that is needed to deter the slugs from attacking prize plants.

Some perennials, for example

Michelmas daises suffer from mildew. If they are affected, treat the plants with a fungicide, following the manufacturer's advice, and take care not to wet other nearby plants with it.

KEEPING THE BORDER LOOKING GOOD

In the first year, you will be eager to see the plants grow quickly to cover the soil and fill in the spaces between plants. But even in the first growing season there will be work that needs doing on the plants. Once blooms are spent, unless they are followed by attractive seedpods that will extend the ornamental attributes of the plant, deadhead the flowering perennials and annuals to keep a succession of blooms going.

Some perennials such as delphiniums and phlox can be cut back after the first flush of flowers. This encourages the growth of sideshoots and a second flowering on these later developing shoots.

If you do not want plants to self-seed, you will need to nip out the seedheads in any case. But if you do not mind taking pot-luck, self-sowing – although it produces copious plants – also produces very pretty effects.

In autumn, once the perennials have finished flowering and you have enjoyed their seedheads, it is best to cut down the spent foliage and stems, so that the border looks tidy. Leave in place the top growth of plants that are not always hardy. The top growth seems to protect the crowns of the plants from the cold. The frost will also make a variety of delightful patterns on the spent growth and this offers an ornamental bonus.

LIFTING AND DIVIDING

Once the border plants are growing well they will spread and enlarge to make good-sized clumps. As they get larger, their flowering vigour may diminish, so every two to three years it is worth lifting the clump and dividing or splitting it up. Replant several of the divisions and the new plants will grow and flower with new energy.

MOVING AN ESTABLISHED SHRUB

1 Quite large shrubs can be moved with care. Move deciduous shrubs when they are dormant. Evergreens are best moved in the autumn or spring. If the plant has spreading or prickly branches, tie them into an upright position.

2 If the shrub is large, it may be necessary to reduce the size of the ball of soil to be lifted. Use the fork to remove more soil, being careful to damage the roots as little as possible.

3 When the root ball looks as if it is a manageable size, use a spade to cut underneath it. Work around the plant evenly from all sides.

4 Make sure the new planting hole has already been dug and is large enough. Then roll up a piece of hessian or tough plastic sheeting, and position it against the root ball. Tilt the plant back and push the wrapping material under it, rocking the root ball back over it.

5 Tie the hessian around the root ball, making sure it is secure. Unless the shrub is small, lifting it will be a job for at least one extra pair of hands. Get help before lifting if necessary.

6 Carefully lower the shrub into the prepared hole. Make sure the shrub will be at its previously planted level, then carefully remove the wrapping material. After filling in the hole and firming the soil, water thoroughly. Continue watering in dry spells for at least several months.

TRANSPLANTING

If a plant is in the wrong place, you may have to live with it for the growing season, but in autumn or spring, you can lift it and move it to a better position.

Spring border

Freshness and vitality are the keynotes of spring borders. Bright yellow narcissi, white and green-tipped snowdrops, soft mauve crocuses and the rainbow colours of tulips are all popular choices.

Regularity and uniformity of planting are often associated with spring schemes. Tulips or narcissi rise high on their long stems above a mass of frothy bedding plants such as forget-me-not, *Myosotis*. It is as if we are imposing a strict management on the waywardness of what are essentially garden versions of wild spring flowers, tamed through intensive breeding programmes for our borders.

Here in the garden recreated at the home of the French Impressionist painter, Monet, in Giverny, France, that regularity and single-minded planting of just two or three different plants provides a sense of infinite space, as well as infinite resources of labour and finance.

The soft-coloured gravel of the hard landscaping in the path defines the border edges clearly. The main plant choices offer a unity of colour and continue the regularity established by the path. Their varying heights and flower colours, though, relieve the monotony of this uniform look and make for a natural rhythm. Edging the long lines of the beds, and making a soft line with the path is the low-growing, mound-forming favourite of spring, *Lobularia maritima* 'Royal Carpet'. Its curved outline spills out of the bed and softens the edge of the path, linking it with the planting.

Soft, billowy white and pale blue, tall bearded iris flowers float high above their angular, lance-like leaves in spring, imitating some exotic butterfly. Before the flowers appear, the fresh green and uniform shape of the foliage plays its own part in the border's overall look. Making a softer contrast are the more natural-looking flowers of the Siberian wallflower, *Erysimum hieraciifolium*, on the left of the path, and the scented wallflower, *Cheiranthus cheiri* on the right. Both are perennials, but in spring bedding schemes they are treated as annuals.

Above: *In contrast to the regularity of the spring border at Giverny, a more natural effect is achieved by the mass planting of spring-flowering bulbs and perennials. Here purple crocus and yellow aconites show their faces above the marbled leaves of Arum italicum pictum, while the rich mauve flowers of hellebores stand atop their leafless stems. In the background are green-tipped white bells of snowdrops.*

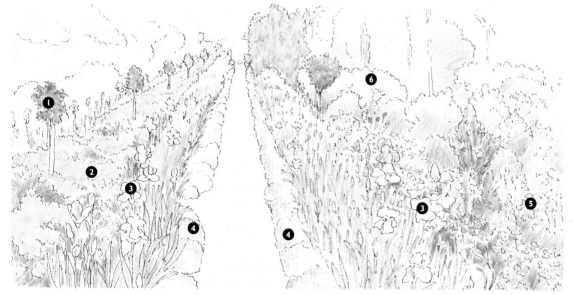

PLANT LIST		
1 Standard roses		
2 *Erysimum hieraciifolium*		
3 Tall bearded iris in blue and white		
4 *Lobularia maritima* 'Royal Carpet'		
5 *Cheiranthus cheiri*		
6 *Hesperis matronalis*		

Adding to the perfume of the wallflowers is the white-flowered form of dame's violet, *Hesperis matronalis,* with its head of massed small flowers. Once their flowers are over, they may seed, but will probably be cut back to allow the leafy rosettes to establish well for the following year's flowering.

To give the border height, there are regularly-spaced and very trimly-shaped standard hybrid tea roses that will flower on their round pom-pom-shaped heads in summer. All these plants, with their different colours and very different shapes and heights, planted out so repetitively, present a seemingly infinite perspective. Later, when the spring flush of flowering is over in this long border, the lobularia flowers will be cut off, probably in a back-breaking shearing over with secateurs, and once it has recovered, the foliage will continue to edge the path.

The iris stems and foliage will have to be cut back to a traditional fan shape. The iris root or rhizome which rests just on the soil surface, will be able to bake in the summer sun, unshaded by the foliage of other plants, building up its resources for future spring flowering. The scented wallflower in this border is treated as an annual spring bedding plant; it will later be replaced by a similar summer bedding plant.

Below: Lobularia maritima *'Royal Carpet' spills across the gravel path, tall bearded blue and white iris, and a fragrant mass of Siberian wallflowers, scented wallflowers and* Hesperis matronalis *provide the spring colour within the border.*

Summer border

Flowers that make pools of colour and shafts of sunlight over a long period are the most popular choice for pleasing effects in a stately summer border. To achieve this there is a wide choice of herbaceous perennial and annual material.

Using plants that offer either vertical or horizontal colour, you can vary the pace of the border's planting. Here the wide, flat heads of closely-packed flowers of *Achillea* 'Cloth of Gold' sway on long stalks above the felt-like, slightly aromatic leaves to make a burst of sunlight-yellow. The streak of yellow is repeated through the border, sometimes with similar plantings of achillea or with sunny-coloured but differently shaped flowers, such as those of *Verbascum* 'Gainsborough'. The candelabra-like flower stems of the verbascum offer a different shape, but a similar block of

colour, and make a break between the busier or more varied colours and hues of its neighbouring plants.

Lowering the height, and thus the focal level, is a swathe of salmon and rosy pink Peruvian lilies, *Alstroemeria ligtu* hybrids. Lily-like, and with their foliage playing hardly any part in the planting, they tumble forwards in the border, separating the yellows and blues. Just as you have taken in the change of height, it rises again, this time with the stately mauve-pink flowers of *Salvia turkestanica* and the deep blue of *Delphinium* 'Fenella'. Holding the line of the

blue flowers, but moving lower in height are clumps of borage and the starry blue of *Anchusa*. *Papaver* 'Mrs Perry', with shapely foliage, holds the front of the border at this point.

The continuity of colour and rhythmic alteration of height hold your attention and demand you shift your gaze, but at a measured and relaxed pace.

A herbaceous border, such as this, can never be described as low maintenance, as there is always a plant that needs deadheading, tying back or staking. Achillea and delphinium in particular should be staked, especially in exposed sites. It is

best to put the stakes or supports in place at the planting time or in spring each year, before the plants have begun to grow away. Then, when they do need the support, they will have grown into it and you will hardly see that it is there.

At its best between June and September, a summer herbaceous border is packed with more than just the plants you can see at any one moment during the season. This allows for some to come to maturity, and then when their blooms are spent, their place is taken, centre stage, by a plant that has been waiting in the wings.

PLANT LIST
1 *Achillea* 'Cloth of Gold'
2 *Verbascum* 'Gainsborough'
3 *Delphinium* 'Fenella'
4 *Salvia turkestanica*
5 *Papaver* 'Mrs Perry'
6 *Anchusa azurea*
7 *Alstroemeria ligtu* hybrids
8 *Penstemon* 'Sour Grapes'
9 *Salvia uliginosa*
10 *Gaura lindheimeri*

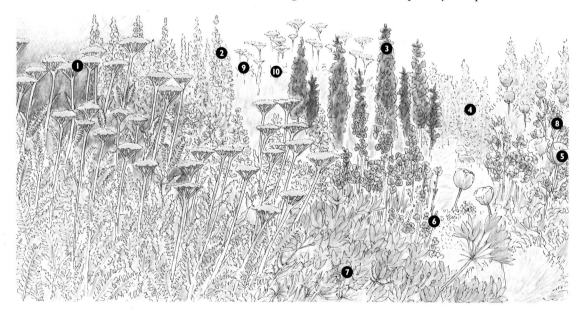

In this border the dancing blue flowers of *Salvia uliginosa* and the delicate, butterfly-like flowers of *Gaura lindheimeri,* wait their turn at the base of giant cardoons, planted through the border. To hold the blues and white of the flowers, and combine them with the grey of the cardoon foliage, *Penstemon* 'Sour Grapes', sparkles to life at the front of the border.

Below: Achillea *'Cloth of Gold' and* Verbascum *'Gainsborough' provide the sunlight, while lighter shades of mauve come from* Salvia turkestanica *and* Papaver *'Mrs Perry', making softer accents. Deep blue blocks of colour are the offerings of* Delphinium *'Fenella' and* anchusa, *while a flame of salmon and rosy pinks light the front of the border.*

Autumn border

As late summer turns into mellow autumn, the colours in the border seem to imitate the tawny colours of foliage, russet fruits and orange vegetables. Even the glow of autumn sunsets and misty early mornings finds an echo in the border.

One group of flowers in particular that fills the colour gap between summer and winter comes from the daisy family – *Compositae*. Once known under such familiar names as chrysanthemum, they now belong to several genera whose names are as mellifluous and honeyed to roll off the tongue as the season itself. Dendranthema, argyranthemum and aster are among their number, with a range of bronze, yellow, mauve, white and ruddy flowers. The most important contribution this range of perennials makes to the autumn border is to maintain colour and interest for as long as possible beyond the full splendour of summer.

Mostly hardy, this group of flowers needs full sun or part-shade to grow well. Well-drained, enriched soil is best for them, but in dry summer seasons, they will need watering to prevent fungal outbreaks. With many species and cultivars growing to a considerable height and carrying flowers on every stem, they are bulky characters that need space for their tawny display to look its best. To keep them from flopping forward dramatically, they should be supported early on in their growing season.

Flowering over a long period, they need deadheading regularly, with their stems cut back to allow for new flowers on shorter spurs. Asters with their smaller, less densely packed flowerheads make a soft focus. In this planting, penstemons, the butterfly-attracting *Sedum x spectabile* 'Brilliant' and the hybrid Japanese anemone, *Anemone x hybrida* 'Bressingham Glow', relieve the emphasis on asters and dendranthema.

Some forms of Michaelmas daisy, such as the modern *Aster novi-belgii* hybrids, are prone to mildew and insect attack and will need regular spraying with a fungicide. If the plants suffer badly, it is best to cut out affected stems, water well and continue the spraying regime.

Here they are planted together in a border that is more a demonstration garden, showing the range of colours available. In your own border, they can be combined and colour-coordinated with other late-flowering autumn dazzlers including the white-flowered

PLANT LIST
1 *Anemone x hybrida* 'Bressingham Glow'
2 *Dendranthema* 'Shining Light'
3 *Aster amellus* 'Jacqueline Genebrier'
4 *Penstemon* 'Thorn'
5 *Dendranthema* 'White Gloss'
6 *Aster lateriflorus* 'Datschii'
7 *Dendranthema* 'Doris'
8 *Dendranthema* 'Moonlight'
9 *Penstemon* 'Raven'
10 *Aster turbinellus*

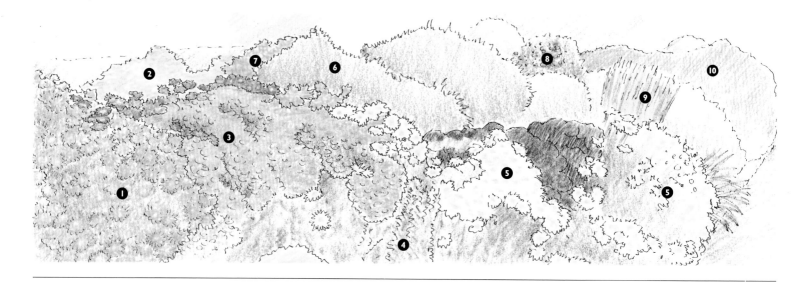

Anemone japonica 'Honorine Jobert' and the sunny yellow-flowered *Rudbeckia* 'Goldsturm'. The white-flowered *Achillea ptarmica* 'The Pearl' and *Campanula lactiflora*, with its branching flower stems in blue, white and sometimes pink blooms, are also good choices to prolong the flowering of the late summer border into autumn.

For the foreground, instead of sedum and penstemon, substitute hostas. *Hosta* 'Honeybells' and *H.* 'Green Fountain' provide particularly glowing foliage and useful flowers. For the background, the tall *Cephalaria gigantea* makes a bold display.

Left: *Their pink-mauve flowers blending so well together, the iceplant* Sedum x spectabile *'Brilliant' and* Dendranthema *'Raquel' provide colour at the front of the border over a long period during the autumn.*

Below: *At the Royal Horticultural Society Garden, Wisley, the late autumn border holds its own mellow display with Japanese anemone, penstemons, dendranthema and asters.*

Winter border

Even in winter's depths there are shrubs and herbaceous perennials that will lighten the gloomiest of days and bring the border to life.

Now that summer and autumnal abundance are past, the border can no longer depend on flowers alone for its richness of colour. Instead, bark, stems, foliage, berries, hips and seedheads, as well as the evergreen framework of hedges, are the factors that impress during this season.

Conifers, in a range of green, gold and even blue needle colour, such as X *Cupresso-cyparis leylandii* 'Castlewellan', together with box, holly, privet and yew, provide the specimen plantings, as well as hedging and edging for the winter garden. But for flaming, glowing colour, the winter stems of dogwood offer the brightest focus. Depending on form, there are stems in many shades of yellow-green and deep red. To ensure that they make the maximum impact, the plants should be stooled or cut back in spring, once their winter display is over. This encourages the growth of new stems throughout the season that will make the display so good the following winter, once their leaves have fallen.

Good stem colour is also available from the ghost bramble, *Rubus cockburnianus* and *Rubus biflorus*, which make a frosty white tracery if planted in the border. The stems should be cut back in spring to encourage new growth, and to keep the plants in hand, although the ghost bramble is not as vigorous as the hedgerow bramble.

If there is space in the garden for trees, within or near the border, maples and birches offer a wonderful range of bark colours and textures.

In a winter border, the most important effect is that of light. In this border, the glow of ground-hugging ivy, *Hedera helix* 'Sagittifolia Variegata', lights the foreground. Moving upwards, the flower bracts of *Helleborus foetidus* take the brightness above their glossy, toothed leaves to the linear stems of the dogwoods, *Cornus alba* 'Sibirica' and *C. stolonifera* 'Flaviramea'.

For floral effects, winter-flowering heaths, such as *Erica* x *darleyensis* 'Darley Dale' or

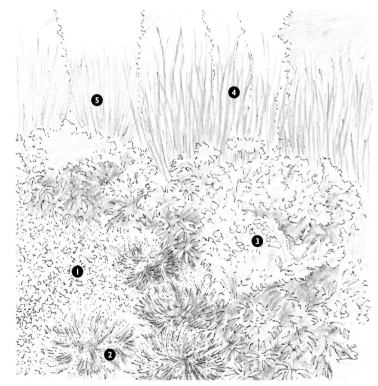

Left: *Flaming fiery colours of witch hazel*, Hamamelis x intermedia *'Jelena' are criss-crossed by the frosty stems of the ghost bramble*, Rubus biflorus. *In the foreground the little blue stem grass makes its autumn red foliage display, while* Erica x darleyensis *and winter-flowering aconites*, Eranthis hyemalis *provide the floral effects.*

Opposite: *In the foreground, the variegated foliage of* Hedera helix *'Sagittifolia Variegata' makes a light carpet for* Erica carnea *'C.J. Backhouse'. Rising in a shimmering row above their dark green shining foliage, the flower bracts of* Helleborous foetidus *take the glowing colour effect to the linear stems of two dogwoods. The light lemon-green of* Cornus stolonifera *'Flaviramea' and the red stems of* Cornus alba *'Sibirica' should be cut to ground level in spring to ensure a good growth of new stems for next winter's show.*

PLANT LIST

1 *Hedera helix* 'Sagittifolia Variegata'
2 *Erica carnea* 'C.J. Backhouse'
3 *Helleborus foetidus*
4 *Cornus alba* 'Sibirica'
5 *Cornus stolonifera* 'Flaviramea'

E. carnea 'C.J. Backhouse' with slightly differing mauve bell-shaped flowers, provide good ground cover and colour at the base of trees and in the foreground of a border.

Small trees and shrubs that carry the floral effect through the season are useful in the border. The pink flowers of *Prunus* x *subhirtella* 'Autumnalis' float across this border, to make a high level floral focus. In the border there are many winter-flowering viburnums such as *Viburnum* x *bodnantense* with its fragrant flowers. For the most dazzling effects of all, witch hazels offer a sparkling firework display with their finely cut flowers in shades of orange, bronze and yellow.

Grasses, too, offer good colour in winter. Some, such as the little blue stem grass, *Schizachyrium scoparium*, have foliage and stems that change colour. The spring and summer blue-green of this grass's stems and foliage turns red in autumn and winter, and if planted fairly densely, will make a strong impact in an informal border.

Incidental effects are also part of the winter display. Seedheads, foliage, stems and evergreen hedging and edging are all transformed into a winter wonderland when the first frost occurs. Then the real bones and framework of the garden are highlighted by a delicate, but ephemeral tracery, that disappears as the winter sun warms the day.

Damp sun

With large lush foliage and flower stems reaching for the sky, plants that enjoy the moisture of a damp sunny site make a dense and luxuriant effect from spring through to late autumn.

No site, nor any conditions, need be a problem to the modern border gardener. Although there are optimum sites and conditions, if you are able to see the garden as a series of natural habitats, then you can accommodate the plants that suit those conditions.

An ancient pond site, filled in centuries ago, but still staying damp for much of the year, is the natural home for plants that are often grown as waterside marginals at the damp edges of ponds. Here, there is no visible water feature, but the plants, with their lush foliage and watery associations, offer the sense of a secret pool. Even though this site is naturally moist for most of the year, it may dry out in a dry summer, like many natural water courses. It will then need watering to maintain the moisture level that the plants enjoy.

By choosing the plants that suit the conditions and site, routine maintenance is cut down. There is still some work that needs to be done, but by suiting the style of gardening, it can be managed on ecological lines. Flowerheads need to be removed once flowering is over, and then stems and foliage can be left as a habitat for wildlife over the winter. In spring, remaining stems, foliage and

Above: *In spring, a damp border is enlivened by the mixed colours of* Primula japonica *seedlings.*

PLANT LIST

1 *Iris sibirica* (here only foliage, not yet in bloom)
2 *Astilbe* 'Fanal'
3 *Ligularia wilsoniana* (not yet in flower)
4 *Primula bulleyana*
5 *Mimulus guttatus*
6 *Rodgersia pinnata* (leaves)
7 *Ligularia* 'The Rocket'
8 *Hosta fortunei* (foliage and flowers)
9 *Artemisia lactiflora*
10 *Filipendula ulmaria* 'Variegata'
11 *Sinacalia tanguticus* (was *Senecio tanguticus*, not yet in flower)

seedheads are cut down and then chopped into small pieces to form a recycled self-mulching material. Dropped into place on the soil surface, they add nutrients and improve the texture of the soil.

In this planting, the large clumps of moisture-loving plants need little staking, as they support themselves. Smaller plants such as astrantias, which are planted near the front of the damp border, need to be staked in early spring. Hazel twigs make a perfect natural-looking support system for them, and are soon covered by the spring growth of the plants.

Much of the hard work of border maintenance is, in fact, done by the plants themselves. First, by supporting themselves, and second, because they make such good ground cover, they suppress weeds and act as their own mulch, to conserve water on the soil surface.

Although at its best over a long flowering period, the damp border has much to offer from its early spring foliage. Hostas, ligularia, iris, astilbe and rodgersia make strong growth in the spring, with their foliage developing and unfurling, full of the promise of the mature plant. Even in lower temperatures they seem to double in size daily, covering the ground and filling the gardener with expectations of the summer to come.

Below: Iris sibirica, *with its lance-like foliage, and* Hosta fortunei, *with grey-blue foliage, make a good contrast in the foreground. The almost all-year round damp nature of the site makes this a perfect setting for moisture-loving plants including astilbe, ligularia and mimulus.*

Dry sun

In a dry, sunny site, it is hot and it feels like the temperature is getting higher all the time. To gain the maximum effect in such a site you will need to find the plants that are at their best in full sun.

With annual bans on watering and use of sprinklers, plants that can perform well in dry sunny conditions offer a bonus beyond their ornamental attractions. Their rich and warm colours keep the visual temperature up, and in this border, the existing dry and sunny conditions have been exploited still further with the addition of the river of gravel paths and walkways. Gravel has also been added to the plantings because it can work as a weed-suppressing and water-retaining mulch.

Visually, the effect is accentuated by the way the plants are grouped together, making islands of flowing colour, rising out of what is an artful creation of a dry river bed. The key to the success of such a planting is the initial preparation and the choice of the right plants. When digging over the site in autumn, it is important to add bulky organic material (as well as channels of grit to improve drainage) to aerate the soil and increase its microscopic water-holding capacity.

When planting, make sure that the plants are watered in well. For a time, while they are establishing you may need to continue to water, but later the plants will have to prove their drought-resistant capacity. Once the plants are in place, the gravel mulch can be spread around them to merge with the gravel in the pathways. By merging the gravel mulch with that of the pathways, a sense of informality and unity is achieved. The plants can spill out over the gravel, adding their own outlines and definition to the sunny border.

Grasses, such as *Miscanthus sinensis* 'Silberspinne' and the lower-growing *Stipa tenuissima,* with their silky, natural-looking panicles, move in the wind to create a rhythmic effect – almost replacing the missing water of the dry gravel bed. By using plants that produce a variety of shapes, such as mounds of low-growing thymes and flowing will-o-the-wisp grasses, you can continue the emphasis on movement of eye and interest. The effect of movement also cools down the high heat of the baking gravel and hot-country plants such as lavender, red hot pokers and fleshy sedums. Good solid blocks of colour combine to form dense plantings of the blue-flowered *Caryopteris clandonensis* 'Heavenly Blue'. They also make a good foil for spikier plants such as the lemon-yellow of *Kniphofia* 'Little Maid'.

In this border there is a regular succession of plants coming into play for foliage, flowers and then seedheads.

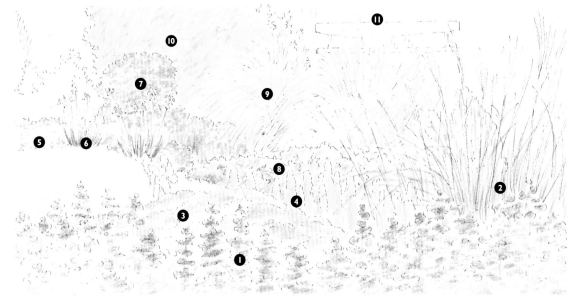

PLANT LIST

1 *Caryopteris clandonensis* 'Heavenly Blue'
2 *Miscanthus sinensis* 'Silberspinne'
3 *Sedum x spectabile* 'Brilliant'
4 *Kniphofia* 'Little Maid'
5 *Sedum x* 'Ruby Glow'
6 *Tulbaghia violacea*
7 *Sedum telephium* 'Atropurpureum'
8 *Euphorbia myrsinites*
9 *Stipa tenuissima*
10 *Nicotiana langsdorffii*
11 *Lavatera* 'Barnsley'

Management of those plants that self-seed copiously is made easier by the gravel. It is much easier to lift seedlings of attractive grasses such as *Stipa tenuissima* and to limit plants that spread by underground runners, when they have rooted into the gravel surface, rather than more solidly into the soil beneath. Large architectural plants such as grey cardoons, *Cynara cardunculus,* are left after flowering to become a faded and even drier part of the garden in dry sun.

Below: *Separated by a gravel pathway, creating the effect of a dry river bed, sun-loving plants rise up and spill out to make waves of colour.*

Dry shade

For the most natural-looking border in difficult dry and shady conditions, treat the area as a natural woodland and woodland edge.

In the garden, dry shade is the predominant condition under evergreen trees or next to conifer hedges. To make such a border work well and be attractive at all times of the year, you need to do some initial site clearing of the trees, especially if they are free-standing (as opposed to being planted as a hedge). Laurels, for example, that have been allowed to grow too large over the years, will darken the ground at their base and deprive any plants growing at the base of light and sufficient water. Two things will improve the chances for growing a wider range of plants successfully in such dry conditions.

First, remove as much of the lower level of branches as you can without leaving the trees looking unsightly. This lightens the ground area. Second, take out some of the branches that form the crown of the tree. Once again, this will allow more light into the scene, but both measures also allow rain to penetrate directly into the ground, and this gives the plants greater resources. You can also improve the soil structure and moisture-holding capacity by adding bulky organic material.

To keep the natural look to a woodland border like the one featured here, give it a curved edge. To get the right curves, lay a hose in place and then cut out the edge, using a sharp spade or an edging tool.

The best plants for a dry shady situation are those that would grow well in the same position in a natural woodland setting. Ground-hugging, mat-forming or scrambling plants that establish quickly and cover a large surface area are the best solution. Species geranium, ivy and ajuga are among the best choices for this.

When the plants are establishing they will need additional water and this may also be necessary during the growing season, especially if there is a drought at that time. If you can afford more permanent watering facilities, install a porous or leaky hose system. The slow, sustained trickle of water will benefit the plants in their establishment and also in their subsequent growth.

Plant them in sufficient quantities starting about 20cm (8in) in from the edge of the bed. The plants will soon spread to cover the bare areas at the centre of the planting and will have the space at the front to spread forwards to the curved edge. Any that spill further over the border edge than you want them to, can be lifted and replanted elsewhere, or simply sliced off with a sharp spade. Otherwise, if you have the space, allow the plants to make their own spread and add to the natural look of the planting. When the clumps become too large and dense, you can reduce their size by lifting and dividing in spring or autumn.

PLANT LIST
1 *Ajuga reptans* 'Jungle Beauty'
2 *Geranium magnificum*
3 *Geranium pratense* 'Flore Pleno'
4 *Deutzia kalmiflora*
5 *Rubus* 'Flore Pleno'
6 *Geranium macrorrhizum* 'Album'
7 *Colchicum autumnale* (leaves)
8 *Arum italicum* (leaves)
9 *Myosotis*
10 *Milium effusum* 'Bowles Gold'
11 *Helleborus sternii* hybrids
12 *Geranium macrorrhizum*
13 *Asperula*

Above: *Curved edges are emphasized when the plants spill across the natural-looking paths in a woodland planting.*

Clay border

Clay soil has the unpleasant characteristic of being wet and sticky in wet weather and baked hard in hot weather. Most gardeners go to great lengths to alter the structure of a clay soil, so that they can grow a wider range of plants.

However, if the clay soil is amended so that its drainage is improved, it can be a highly fertile soil, since the tightly packed clay particles hold nutrients and moisture that are available to the plant in a well-balanced clay.

The best way to improve a clay soil is by incorporating bulky organic matter in early autumn and late spring, when the soil is workable. If waterlogging is a problem the soil will require better drainage – either by digging in grit or, more expensively, installing drainage channels. If you are starting to make a border from scratch on a clay soil, its soil pH may need altering as sometimes clay soils can be quite acid, especially when they are waterlogged and moss grows on the surface.

To reduce the acidity and sweeten the soil, lime is often applied, but only to ground that is clear of plants and that can be dug and left over a long period in autumn and winter. Never apply lime at the same time as you add fertilizer to the soil, as the lime causes the fertilizer to break down too quickly. In an ornamental border, where a range of plants can be grown, liming is probably not necessary, unless you are renovating or making a new border. It might be more important in a vegetable garden where

production rather than ornament is the aim.

Once there is better drainage and the soil's fertility is improved, the range of plants that can be grown is wider than if you had simply left it unaltered. Generally, those that tolerate a clay soil are also plants that grow well in moist marginal, waterside plantings, such as astilbe, phormium, hosta, houttuynia, lysimachia, *Gunnera manicata* and rodgersia. Shrubs that do well on clay are dogwoods, philadelphus, *Viburnum opulus* and berberis.

Phormiums may need winter protection in cold areas. This can be provided by wrapping the plants in a conifer blanket of cut branches forced into the ground and tied around the plant with

PLANT LIST

1 *Lavandula* species
2 *Salvia officinalis*
3 *Rosa* 'Marjorie Fair'
4 *Gaura lindheimeri*
5 *Phlox paniculata*
6 *Phlox maculata*
7 *Hosta sieboldiana* 'Elegans'
8 *Rosa* 'Flower Carpet'
9 *Acanthus hungaricus*
10 *Thalictrum aquilegiifolium*
11 *Nicotiana sylvestris*
12 *Crambe cordifolia*
13 *Phytostegia virginiana* 'Crown of Snow'
14 *Papaver somniferum*
15 *Phormium tenax* 'Sundowner'

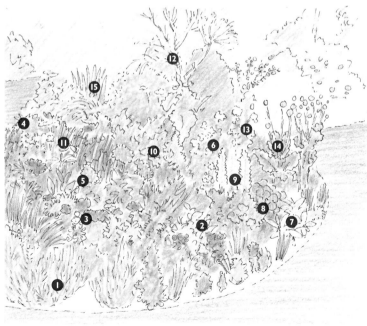

string to secure them well.

Roses, too, are more tolerant of clay than many plants, and in a border that has been well-prepared and enriched, a more or less traditional scheme with roses and herbaceous underplanting can be achieved.

At the planting stage, water the plants in well and in dry seasons see that the border is well-watered. A mulch of bark chippings or leaf mould will help to conserve soil moisture, and this should be set in place in spring, when the soil has begun to warm up. The mulch will also help warm the cold clay soil.

Opposite: *In the hot colour corner of this border,* Ligularia *'The Rocket',* Crocosmia *'Lucifer' and* Rudbeckia sullivantii *'Goldsturm' provide the heat, while a purple-leaved* Phormium tenax *makes a strong colour contrast.*

Above: *In this amended clay soil, the plants that in any case tolerate clay, such as roses, phormium and astilbe, do well, but there are more that can be included in the planting once the soil is improved.*

Acid soil

Sumptuous spring blooms of camellias and rhododendrons are the treasures that can be offered by borders on acid soil, while raised peat beds provide just the right site for alpines that thrive on an acid soil.

If the site is too large to attempt to sweeten or lower the acidity of the soil, there is much to be enjoyed year-round from the range of plants, although limited, that will survive the acid soil's pH level of below 5.5. These plants will tolerate the lack of lime and can cope with the sourness and acidity of the conditions. Known as lime-haters they include azaleas, camellias, rhododendrons, heathers and many woody shrubs, and in many gardens where the pH is neutral or alkaline, special peat beds are constructed to grow some of the choice lime-hating plants.

Usually designed as a terraced or raised bed and made from peat blocks, a peat bed is filled with peaty soil and lined at its base to prevent any contact with the alkaline soil from the rest of the garden. It should be in a semi-shaded site to avoid too much water loss.

Before you use peat blocks, soak them in water and let them drain. Then you can begin to build the raised bed or terraces. If you are using them to make a rectangular raised bed, put them in place as you would bricks and then keep them in place with canes pushed down through the whole peat wall at intervals.

Below: *Banks of flowers in spring and attractive foliage year-round are the splendid ornamental attributes of a rhododendron planting of great size.*

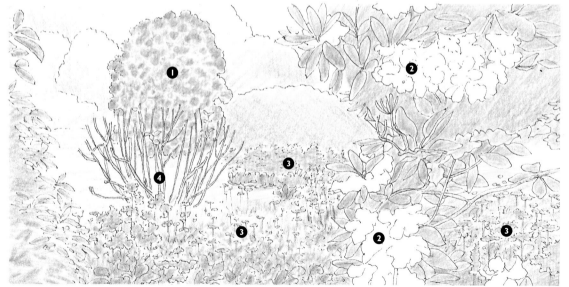

PLANT LIST

1 *Rhododendron* 'Cynthia'
2 *Rhododendron* 'White Diamond'
3 *Primula pulverulenta*
4 *Cornus*

Acid-loving plants
Arbutus
Calluna
Camellia
Corydalis flexuosa
Erica
Fothergilla
Gentiana sino-ornata
Hamamelis
Kalmia
Lithodora diffusa
Magnolia
Pernettya
Pieris nana
Rhododendron, azalea and dwarf rhododendron spp and cultivars

Fill the terraces or raised bed with a peaty compost, or with one of the many peat substitutes now available. Water retention is very important, and any material used should have good water-retaining qualities, such as a fibrous acid loam. Make sure that any material used to infill the bed has a low pH, otherwise the acid-loving plants will not thrive.

As you fill in with the compost, firm the surface well and then water the whole bed and leave it to settle and drain for a day or two. When the peat or peat substitute has settled, position the plants and plant them up. Once the plants are in place, they will need regular watering while they establish in the first growing season. Spread a layer of bark chippings on the surface and around the plants for a weed-suppressing mulch.

The peat bed will suit dwarf species of rhododendrons and cultivars, a wide range of alpine plants including *Lithodora diffusa, Pieris nana, Gentiana sino-ornata, Corydalis flexuosa* and other species of primula. Roses will do well in acid soils, but they prefer a pH level closer to neutral, around 5.5-6.5.

For the larger shrubs and rhododendrons, adopt the same principle as the peat bed, but use a liner to separate alkaline soil from the acid contents of the bed. You may have to be content with growing azaleas, camellias and rhododendrons in large containers with ericaceous compost. Container-grown lime-haters need regular annual doses of sequestered iron.

Below: Rhododendron *'Cynthia' and 'White Diamond' in the foreground frame a moist, grassy glade where naturalized candelabra primulas,* Primula pulverulenta, *make a stunning display in spring.*

Sandy border

Gardening on light sandy soil has some benefits, but to be able to grow choice plants, some changes have to be made to improve the soil.

A free-draining light soil is one that warms up quickly in spring, but cools down quickly as well, and it dries out, needing frequent watering in dry periods. To make it work better for your border plants you need to add bulky organic material to increase the humus levels. The soil should be fertilized in spring to increase nutrient levels.

Other than this, the easiest solution is to grow those plants that are known to do well on light or poor soils, and those that are grouped together as drought-resistant plants. Most are deep-rooted, so will get their roots well down to where soil moisture is available, but some have special fleshy leaves and stems or grey foliage that either store water or have lower moisture loss through evaporation from the plant itself.

This border, created for the Chelsea Flower Show in London, seems to grow right down to the sandy beach. The grey-leaved shrubby ragwort, *Brachyglottis* 'Sunshine', and the pinkish-red of valerian, *Centranthus ruber,* combine well at the foot of the pavilion.

Sea buckthorn makes a good windbreak and can be trained as a single stem or multi-stem small tree. Provided there is a male tree in the planting, female plants will bear orange berries in autumn in great abundance. In winter, when the plants in the dune planting have died, the buckthorn continues to offer its shapely stems, and the border relies on its own undulations for interest, taking on a more architectural form without the plants.

The other flowers in the planting are essentially cornfield annuals, which grow on a wide range of soils. But to achieve a strong colour block, like the one in this border, you would need to treat them as annual bedding: sowing them into modules, potting on and planting out into enriched and improved soil. If left to self-seed, the colour combinations would become more mixed and random.

The white and mauve flowers of dame's violet, *Hesperis matronalis,* will fill the air with fragrance, especially in the evening. Viper's bugloss, *Echium vulgare,* with its upright blue flower spike, makes a good contrast with the cupped flowers of the cornfield. Below it there is a bank of red-flowered pheasant's eye, *Adonis annua.* This and the yellow-flowered buttercup are more likely to grow in this free-draining situation if the underlying sand is improved beforehand with some manure. Sow seed in spring or autumn into a tray with a good mix of other wild flowers and grasses.

At the edge of the brackish pool in the garden, the bulrush, *Typha latifolia,* makes a strong upright form. Heartsease, *Viola tricolor,* grows at the border's edge, with white campion and

PLANT LIST
1 *Ranunculus acris*
2 *Brachyglottis* 'Sunshine'
3 *Centranthus ruber*
4 *Hesperis matronalis*
5 *Viola tricolor*
6 *Echium vulgare*
7 *Adonis annua*
8 *Typha latifolia*
9 *Hippophae rhamnoides*

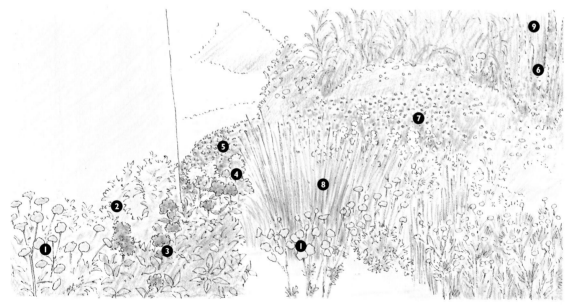

herb Robert, foxgloves and mallows in the more shaded woodland edge. For these plants to grow well in this situation the organic matter levels in the sandy soil need to be increased.

However, there are many plants to choose from that will tolerate the free-draining situation. These include bear's breeches (*Acanthus spinosus*), agapanthus, achillea, alyssum, anaphalis, nepeta and the dune grass, marram. The blue grass, *Festuca glauca*, is also a good choice for such a site. Sun-loving plants such as nepeta and rock roses will make good ground cover and spill from the border onto the path.

Silvery-leaved plants to choose for the border include the giant thistle *Onopordum acanthium* and the spiky-leaved, metallic-blue flowered eryngium. Artemisia, ballota and euphorbias will provide good foliage contrasts with their felt-like textures and, in the case of euphorbias, colourful bracts.

Above: *If your border site is in full sun and on very well-drained soil, there is a wide range of plants to choose from. You could accentuate the seaside feel to it, by growing drought-resistant plants that enjoy the conditions.*

Chalky border

Warm and well-drained, chalk and limestone soils with their high lime and alkaline content, play host to a diverse mix of plants, some with more delicate floral attributes than others, but all repaying close inspection.

Although very different in texture and colour, chalk and limestone soils have a similarly high alkaline content. There is a wide range of plants that will tolerate this high lime content, but for an even richer diversity of species it will be necessary to improve the organic content of the soil. By manuring with compost, green manures and bulky organic material, the drainage and the humus content of the soil will be improved. Fertilizers also help to balance the nutrient levels. Chalk soils tend to be lacking in potash, which must be applied for the plants to do well.

Decidious trees such as *Acer davidii* and *A. rubrum,* grown for their autumn foliage and usually described as lime-tolerant, may not always produce their foliage display on soils with a high alkaline content. Instead, the leaves will shrivel and fall. However, *Sorbus sargentiana, Euonymus alatus* and *E. europaeus,* do produce their brilliant autumnal colours, even on poor soils over chalk.

Grey foliage plants such as dianthus, saxifrage and gypsophila seem to grow well on these soils and offer a softening foliage effect as well as attractive flowers. Mediterranean plants including lavender, santolina, artemisia, helianthemums and cistus also do well in these high alkaline soils, benefiting from the good drainage available.

In the border shown here, set against a limestone wall, the plants chosen to ornament it are tolerant of a wide range of sites, but look particularly attractive spilling away from the wall. Using mound-forming, ground-hugging plants such as Cheddar pink *(Dianthus)*, *Sedum acre* 'Album', *Campanula poscharskyana,* aubrieta and *Thymus doerfleri* in the foreground, and bushy shapes of *Centranthus ruber, Berberis* 'Nana' and *Euonymus* 'Emerald Gaiety' in the background, the border clothes the foot of the wall and presents a simple and natural-looking show.

Chalk soils are usually rather more free-draining than limestone soils, nonetheless there are still plants that will grow well and thrive in them. Deep-rooted plants that can get their roots down into the fissures in the chalky layer will do well. The plants can be helped on their way if the top 60cm (24in) is broken up so that it is not a solid layer.

Among the trees that will do well in borders with high

PLANT LIST
1 *Sedum acre* 'Album'
2 *Euonymus* 'Emerald Gaiety'
3 *Campanula poshcharskyana*
4 *Dianthus gratianopolitanus*
5 *Thymus doerfleri*
6 *Aubretia*
7 *Taxus baccata*
8 *Sisyrinchium striatum*
9 *Betula pendula* 'Young's Weeping'
10 *Berberis* 'Nana'
11 *Helianthemum*
12 *Centranthus ruber*

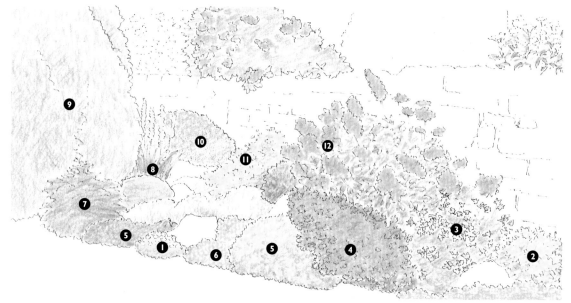

alkalinity are *Sorbus aria, Prunus avium* 'Plena' and *Acer negundo* 'Variegatum'. Shrubs include berberis, *Buddleja davidii, Choisya ternata,* deutzia and philadelphus. Perennials that will be useful in the middle to back of a border include eryngium, *Acanthus spinosus, Achillea filipendulina* 'Gold Plate' and verbascum. For the foreground, use *Scabiosa caucasica* 'Clive Greaves', bergenia and doronicum.

Of the more drought-resistant plants that can grow here, thymes and dianthus are particularly useful in the front of the border. There are also numerous annuals and biennials which you can use, such as *Lavatera trimestris* 'Silver Cup', matthiola, tagetes and many everlasting flowers including *Limonium sinuatum* and *Xeranthemum annuum*.

Below: *Hugging the foot of the wall, mound-forming plants such as* Euonymus *'Emerald Gaiety',* Sedum acre *'Album' and Cheddar pinks make a good background for the pink-red flowerheads of* Centranthus ruber.

White border

Mystical and symbolic in art and literature, white flowers were once prized for their clarity and purity. A border of white flowers, creamy white variegated foliage and silver-leaved plants is both pleasant to walk along and soothing to view.

White is the absence of colour, and yet, in the garden, against green foliage and grass and blue sky, it can sometimes be very dominating, especially on tall flower spikes of foxgloves and delphiniums. White has several "shades" and textures – it can be silvery and metallic, waxy, milky, creamy and even, with a hint of another colour, a blush-white. In a hot summer border, full of brightly-coloured flowers, a group of white blooms or silver foliage will act as a cooling agent and dampen down the over-heated colours of other plants.

In every season there is a wide range of plants with white blooms: in spring, snowdrops, the white grape hyacinth, *Muscari azureum* 'Album', the white Dutch hyacinth 'Carnegie', *Iris magnifica,* white crocus, tulips and even *Narcissus* 'Empress of Ireland', will provide colour into early summer. Summer-flowering bulbs including fragrant *Lilium candidum, L. regale* and *L. longiflorum* take you further into the growing season. *Cyclamen hederifolium* 'Album' flowers in autumn, together with the white-flowered autumn crocus, *Colchicum speciosum* 'Album'. Many spring-flowering trees and shrubs offer showers of white blooms, that later make a ground level performance as their petals fall.

Most border perennials have a white or almost white form, so the choice is wide. Peonies, lupins, phlox, campanulas, delphiniums, hardy geraniums and irises all have lovely white varieties. In spring, *Dicentra spectabilis* 'Alba' and even the herb, sweet Cicely offer attractive white flowers for the shady border. Late in the season, *Anemone* x *hybrida* makes a good display and for the largest cloud of white, rising above the border, use *Crambe cordifolia,* with its mass of tiny flowers.

Shrubs and climbers for a white border include the white-flowered *Magnolia salicifolia, Clematis armandii,* climbing roses *Rosa* 'Iceberg' and *R.* 'Mme Alfred Carrière'.

At night, the white border is particularly tranquil as the tall spires of flowers seem to stand out from the shadows of dusk. At this time, the fragrance of the *Nicotiana sylvestris* drifts through the air. Annuals for the white border include *Lavatera trimestris* 'Silver Cup', the white form of love-in-a-mist and sweet peas. There is a white form of the perennial sweet pea which looks good when planted to climb up a cane wigwam.

At ground level, the silver-streaked dead nettle, *Lamium* 'White Nancy' or 'Album' makes good ground cover in the spring, but the pink flowers may not fit the colour scheme later on. Variegated foliage of hostas and ivy are also useful for lighting up shady areas.

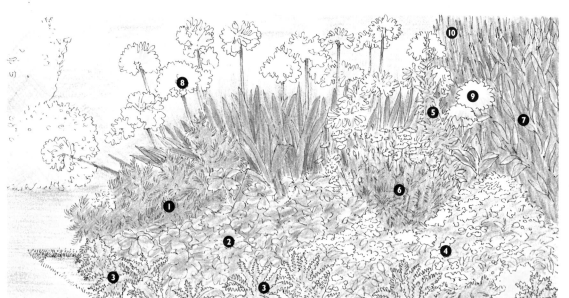

PLANT LIST
1 Artemisia
2 *Astrantia major*
3 *Senecio maritimus*
4 *Anaphalis triplinervis*
5 *Artemisia ludoviciana*
6 *Anthemis punctata*
7 *Prunus laurocerasus* 'Otto Luyken'
8 *Agapanthus campanulatus* 'Albidus'
9 *Dahlia* 'Nymphenberg'
10 *Juniperus* 'Blue Spire'

The most celebrated white garden is that created by Vita Sackville-West (Lady Nicholson) at Sissinghurst in Kent, England, in the late 1930s. Enclosed within walls of well-clipped yew hedges, its whiteness is pure and tranquil. It has had many imitators and some detractors, who claim that the unrelenting whiteness of the planting is boring. It is hard, though, to plant a completely white border, since stamens, nectar guide marks and stems also play a part in the overall look, and add to the interest. One problem associated with a white garden, is that once flowering is over, and also after rain, the blooms turn yellow and brown and only constant cutting back and deadheading improves the look.

Right: *Although many of the flowers in the planting are white and creamy-yellow, variegations in the foliage make for a more interesting colour effect.*

Below: *Silver-leaved plants, including* Senecio maritimus *and artemisia, add a soft focus and seem to anchor the tall stems of* Agapanthus campanulatus *'Albidus'.*

45

Yellow border

Golden shades of clear bright yellow through slightly tangy orange are the glowing colours that lighten the border. They work well when planted in groups, or even as the predominant colour in a sunny border.

Using a limited range of colours you can achieve a very bright and bold effect. Here, the border to the side of a curved path is planted with a predominantly yellow to orange colour scheme. This lightens the path and the lawn edge, and as the plantings are well established they form good clumps, and the blocks of colour repeat at intervals along the border, so taking your eye along with them

Not only do they take your eye with them, but they invite your feet to follow and tread the soft curve of the path to the next delight in the garden. Although as a colour yellow has great vitality and zest, in this particular grouping, the lighter shades – the lemon and cream-yellow – are accentuated, making for a slightly muted tone. *Anthemis tinctoria* 'E.C. Buxton' with its lemon-yellow daisy flowers growing slightly higher than most other plants in this setting, is the plant that makes the strongest impact. Its mass of flowers emphasizes this impact. In the evening light, this particular shade of yellow is almost luminiscent, and the

flowers seem to hang in the air, as their stalks disappear far into the twilight.

The luminescent quality of the planting continues in the use of the metallic-leaved New Zealand daisy, *Celmisia semi-cordata*. Although its spiky leaves look as though they would prefer the heat, it does not do so well in hot dry climates. Grow it in the sun, in humus-rich and well-drained but moist soil.

Taking the colour to orange and back again is a large clump of double Welsh poppies in lemon-yellow and silky-orange. Rising above them and keeping the same dual colour partnership are kniphofias. Among these are *Kniphofia* 'Apricot' and *K. rufa,* with their

orange-yellow flaming torches of flowers. Continuing the metallic theme here is the foliage of *Echinops ritro.* The silvery-blue flowers alter the tempo slightly and with the blue-green leaves of hostas, seem to cool down the sunny vibrance of the yellows and oranges in the border. White is also used as a colour-calming measure, with the tall spires of white foxgloves and the bell-shaped flowers of *Campanula persicifolia.*

Although there are many choice and unusual plants such as the double form of Welsh poppy and the New Zealand daisy, the border is not unapproachable. Strong colour also comes from some simple and familiar plants, such as pot marigold, that can be relied on to provide waves of flowers over a long period throughout the summer season.

The style of the border is informal and flowing, but its division from other, more formal parts of the garden is marked by a well-clipped box pyramid, which acts as a sort of reminder that a different area of the garden is in view.

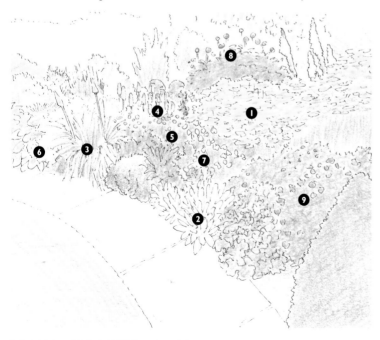

PLANT LIST

1 *Anthemis tinctoria* 'E.C. Buxton'
2 *Celmisia semi-cordata*
3 *Kniphofia rufa*
4 *Kniphofia* 'Apricot'
5 *Meconopsis cambrica*
6 *Hosta* 'Halcyon'
7 *Campanula persicifolia*
8 *Echinops ritro*
9 *Calendula officinalis*

Opposite: *Grouped in substantial clumps, the yellows of* Achillea filipendulina *'Cloth of Gold' and lysimachia appear as shafts of sunlight, running through the border, attracting your eye and attention.*

Below: *Metallic foliage of the New Zealand daisy and* Echinops ritro *help to soothe and calm the bright, sunny nature of the yellow and orange flowers in the predominantly yellow border.*

Red hot border

By late summer, the romantic and sensuous display of roses, lilies and peonies is over. Now in the real heat of summer, some of the most difficult colours to combine come into their own.

One way to beat the heat is by joining it – with an equally hot display of plants with red, orange and sunny yellow flowers. These colours are hard to combine, and with their energetic, frenetic tones – although enjoyable in short bursts – they can hardly be called restful.

Here, strong yellows of *Helianthus* 'Loddon Gold' at the back and *Bidens ferulifolia* at the front of the border make a framework for the hot reds at the centre of this grouping. The tall red hot poker, *Kniphofia* 'Lord Roberts' rises on bare, rather ugly stems, that are here cleverly concealed by the wonderful burgundy-purple foliage of the red-flowered *Dahlia* 'Bishop of Llandaff'.

The hot and dazzling effect is cooled down just a notch by the lemon-green foliage of *Weigela* 'Briant Rubidor' at the edge of the group. To keep this vigorous, prune out old flowering stems to ground level in spring. The half-hardy *Argyranthemum* 'Penny' with its pale lemony-yellow flowers contributes a similar effect. A border with vibrant, bright colours such as these needs a good background planting so that it can flame and sizzle with some impact. Evergreen conifer hedges, or as shown here a purple foliage, *Prunus cerasifera,* make good foils for these colour combinations.

In spring, though somewhat

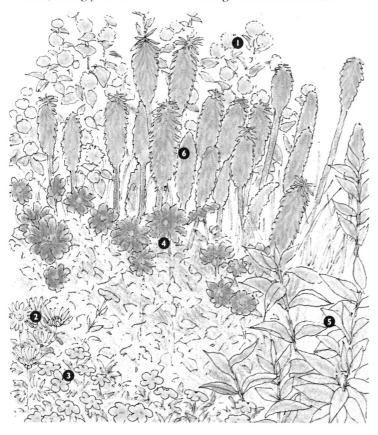

PLANT LIST

1 *Helianthus* 'Loddon Gold'
2 *Argyranthemum* 'Penny'
3 *Bidens ferulifolia*
4 *Dahlia* 'Bishop of Llandaff'
5 *Weigela* 'Briant Rubidor'
6 *Kniphofia* 'Lord Roberts'

Above: *The purple foliage of* Berberis thunbergii 'Atropurpurea', *and that of* Heuchera micrantha *'Palace Purple', act as repeated anchors, and help to coordinate the overall look of this red hot border.*

muted in comparison to the tones of late summer, there are plenty of plants to give a hot look to the border. *Euphorbia griffithii* 'Fireglow' with its posy-like orange bracts makes a strong show, as does the Chilean fire bush *Embothrium coccineum*, although this prefers an acid soil. Orange *Fritillaria imperialis* and bi-coloured orange and golden tulips are some of the dazzlers of the spring bulb border, while in late summer the bird-like plumes of *Crocosmia* 'Lucifer' make an exotic display combined with bright red *Geum* 'Mrs J. Bradshaw' and the fiery red of *Lychnis chalcedonica*.

To achieve a good display, it is necessary to plant closely so that the plants support each other, or at least conceal the artificial supports you may have to put in place, and to suppress competing weeds. Regular hoeing is also a necessary part of the maintenance to keep annual weeds in hand. Deadhead to keep a succession of strong colour going through the season. Half-hardy plants, such as *Argyranthemum* 'Penny' and *Dahlia* 'Bishop of Landaff' will need winter protection. In the case of the argyranthemum, it is best to take cuttings to over-winter for planting next year.

Right: *Framed by a circle of yellow flowers and foliage,* Kniphofia *'Lord Roberts' seems to flame through the border.*

Evergreen border

Flower and foliage colour combine to make the most showy of displays, but plantings that rely on the evergreen foliage of shrubs can offer just as pleasing an effect.

All through the growing season, evergreen plants provide the framework – sometimes as hedging, edging or as a backdrop or screen – for their more colourful border companions. In spring and summer, their individual beauty is often hidden because of the background role they play so well. In winter, they become the shapely and glossy main characters on the garden stage, and in a cold season, their foliage takes on the extra dimension of a frosty rime, that turns them from plants into architectural forms.

There are some plantings that take advantage, in summer and winter, of the interesting and varied leaf shapes and textures that these evergreen plants have. One such planting is in a knot garden, a form that was popular in Tudor and Elizabethan gardens, where the plants are so closely packed and so tightly clipped that they form ribbons of green or grey and make striking patterns.

Evergreen plants are not necessarily green. There are gold and blue forms of conifer, holly with variegated leaves, box with variegated leaves and ivies that can be grown on shapes and clipped into topiary forms, or left to scramble as ground or wall cover. Elaeagnus, camellias, escallonias and holly with glossy green leaves can also be

Above: *A ground-covering planting of* Hebe pinguifolia *'Pagei' makes a good all-year feature. The white stems of the ghost bramble,* Rubus biflorus, *rise through it, as do the burr-like flowers of the New Zealand acaena.*

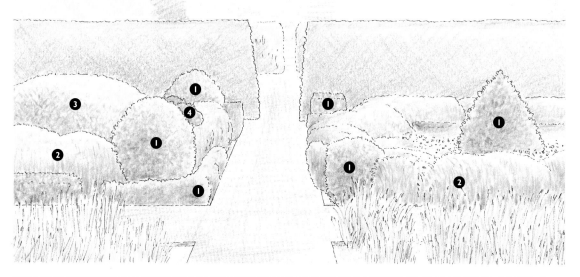

PLANT LIST

1 *Buxus sempervirens*
2 *Santolina chamaecyparissus* 'Nana'
3 *Santolina chamaecyparissus*
4 *Berberis buxifolia* 'Nana'

manipulated into good shapes to add architectural structure to the evergreen border.

Pencil-slim cypresses, thrusting junipers and small-leaved box planted in a border make very definite and shapely statements about the formality of the border's style. Box clipped into pyramids, rounds or cube shapes make well-defined punctuation marks that guide your eye through the

border and, after the flowers are over, they continue to offer a structural element to the border.

In this knot garden, the small outer hedges are of box and the grey-leaved, dwarf form of cotton lavender. The larger form, *Santolina chamaecyparissus* creates the central mound of one of the knot gardens, with a pyramid of box making the other central feature. The purple-leaved *Berberis buxifolia* 'Nana',

although not evergreen, still makes its architectural statement in winter with its purple stems. To maintain the shapes and ribbons of the knot garden, close clipping is required in spring and again in late summer.

Below: *Shapely and structural evergreen shrubs offer colour in grey, green, gold and even blue, throughout the year.*

BORDERS BY FORM

Formal border

The formal look, closely-planted and colourful, is the traditional way to display groups of summer and autumn flowering plants. The rigid way in which the plants are grouped together gives the clues to the formal style of the border.

Two characteristics of a formal border planting are the depth of the border and the way it is set against a backdrop, of either a hedge, as shown here, or of a wall. Here, the low hedge is almost lost next to the imposing brick posts and iron gate that the borders frame. The depth of planting is about 2m (6ft) but many traditional formal borders have a greater depth. This allows for a deep planting where sufficient numbers of plants are arranged to make a very strong impact when they are flowering. Traditionally, there should be enough space between hedge or wall and the back of the border

to enable the gardener to maintain it. The path space also allows for a current of air, something which, if lacking, makes plants susceptible to fungal and other diseases.

In a formal border there is usually a regular gradation of height, with low-growing plants in the foreground and medium to tall plants taking the level back to the wall or hedge backdrop. The plants are grouped in large enough numbers to make a strong colour impact, enhanced by the close planting of the design. Further impact is achieved by repeating plants so that similar

blocks of colour appear along the border. One of the effects of the repeated colour is that it acts as a marker, and takes the viewer by the hand, along the border, almost as if it were a nectar guide for insects in an individual flower.

Such a border is typical of large gardens, where once there were hordes of gardeners involved in its maintenance. And time-consuming maintenance it was, since a formal border is one which needs constant attention. After initial preparation and planting, the plants need a spring mulch with bulky organic matter or compost. They need to

be staked early in the growing season, so that by the time the plants have reached the height of the supports, they have more or less obliterated them.

Annuals such as nicotiana hybrids will be put into the border in spring, to follow the show of plants such as wallflowers and forget-me-not. Lavender, here used as a low-edging plant for the border, has to be clipped after flowering to keep its shape compact. If lavender plants are left, they tend to become woody and leggy, with their centres opening up so that they sprawl rather than edge.

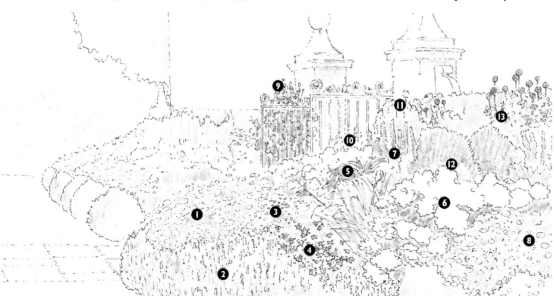

PLANT LIST
1 *Argyranthemum* 'Jamaica Primrose'
2 *Lavandula angustifolia*
3 *Potentilla* 'Gibson's Scarlet'
4 *Nicotiana hybrids*
5 *Hemerocallis* 'Stafford'
6 *Phlox paniculata* 'White Admiral'
7 *Lythrum salicaria*
8 *Erigeron*
9 *Alcea rosea*
10 *Aconitum lycoctonum* spp. *vulparia*
11 *Salvia sclarea*
12 *Aster*
13 *Echinops ritro*

The aim in a formal border is to have colour through the season, beginning with bulbs and spring bedding. The main display comes in the summer and autumn with a wide range of herbaceous perennials, some summer bedding and possibly the inclusion of half-hardy plants such as cannas and the daisy-flowered argyranthemums.

Below: *Two small formal borders frame the imposing posts and iron gate. Edged with lavender, they are colourful throughout the year.*

Island border

Offering a greater challenge to the border gardener, curved island beds that can be viewed from all round the site have become a popular alternative to a traditional, linear formal border.

Unlike the formal border, which is viewed from the front with plants graded from low to tall and planted from front to back, the island border has to have an all-round focus and design.

Although there may be repeats of colour blocks and groupings in an island bed, it is unlikely that it will have as strictly a repeated planting scheme as a traditional formal border.

Instead, depending on the size and shape of the island, there will be two or three groups of taller plants, or even one or two specimen trees or shrubs, set roughly in the central area of the

Opposite: The curved shape and irregular height gradation make an island border less formal. It is challenging to plant in the round – every angle has to hold something of interest for the gardener and the garden visitor.

bed. The other plants will be arranged in sections, following an informal height gradation.

In these borders the height and central interest is achieved by planting ornamental shrubs or trees, stooled to produce multi-stems. For example, *Sambucus nigra* 'Pulvurulenta', a form of elder with its green leaves striped and mottled white, is cut back hard in spring, to encourage growth of stems bearing its attractive foliage. In the border beyond, *Populus serotina* 'Aurea', the golden Italian poplar, is growing as a small bushy tree, but it could be stooled or pollarded to produce stems with its handsome yellow foliage. This poplar turns a yellow-green through the season, until in autumn it produces golden-yellow hues. Both are unusual choices for an island border and they make a distinctive show in the season. In winter, until cut back in spring, their stems make a

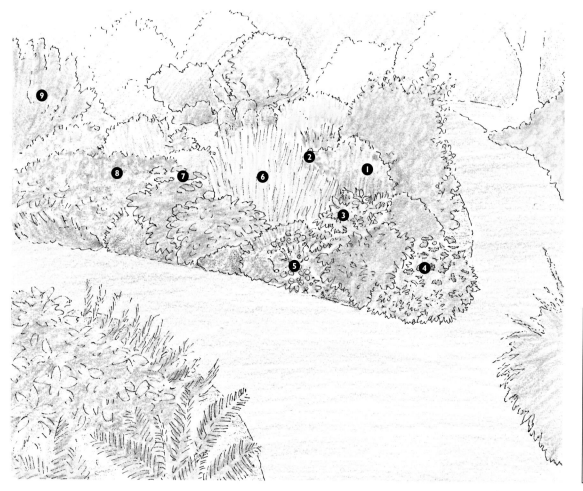

PLANT LIST	
1	*Salvia guaranitica*
2	*Lobelia cardinalis*
3	*Polygonatum hybridum*
4	*Osteospermum jucundum*
5	*Origanum laevigatum* 'Herrenhausen'
6	*Iris pseudacorus* 'Variegata'
7	*Ligularia dentata* 'Desdemona'
8	*Persicaria amplexicaulis* 'Atrosanguinea'
9	*Populus serotina* 'Aurea'

framework for frost patterns if the season is severe.

The floral colour in the island bed comes from plants including the technically half-hardy *Salvia guaranitica*. Here it has proved hardy, but cuttings are taken each year as an insurance policy, and other parts of the garden are filled with this deep blue sage that blooms from late summer till November. Other half-hardy plants include the mauve *Osteospermum jucundum*.

Although some of the half-hardy plants in the bed have survived numberous winters, it is always worth taking cuttings to ensure that you have new plants just in case. Apart from stooling the golden poplar and planting in the half-hardies in late spring to early summer, the border needs deadheading, mulching in spring, and splitting and dividing in autumn to stay in good heart.

Hardy perennials in the island bed include the deep red-flowered and purple foliage *Lobelia cardinalis*, the purple-flowered ornamental marjoram, *Origanum laevigatum* 'Herrenhausen', *Ligularia dentata* 'Desdemona' and *Iris pseudacorus* 'Variegata'

Circular border

Sometimes the form of a border is as breathtaking as the plant combinations that fill it, and here the concept of a border in the round is taken beyond the limits of simply an island of plants.

PLANT LIST

1 *Clematis* 'Victoria'
2 *Miscanthus sinensis* 'Cascade'
3 *Veronica virginica*
4 *Phlox paniculata* 'Elizabeth Arden'
5 *Monarda* 'Balance'
6 *Tradescantia* 'Zwanenburg Blue'
7 *Delphinium* 'Piccolo'
8 *Thalictrum aquelegifolium*
9 *Monarda* 'Scorpion'
10 *Galega hartlandii* 'Lady Wilson'

Above: *One of the many sitting places in the garden has a view over the inner pool area.*

Above: *The inner triangular paths seem to be as curved as the outer path, but it is actually an illusion created by the circular retaining wall and the soft overspilling of the plants.*

The photograph (right) shows a section of a circular border with a concentric circular path going nearly all the way round it. A concentric border, 2m (6ft) deep, planted with colours that correspond to those of the inner circle, lies inside the path. The circles are further emphasized by the 36-pole pergola circle and the circular retaining wall and pond terrace at the centre of the garden. The inner circular border, large in its scope but treated in essence like a long border that has been curved back on itself, is crossed by two sets of paths that make their own contrasting double triangular shape on the design.

On paper, the intellectual geometry of the border is easy to grasp and once it is filled with the plants, combined so well and on so many different levels, the extraordinary harmony and symmetry of the garden reveals an overlay of colour, texture and fragrance. There are nine distinct colour schemes in the inner circle. The starting point for the different colour schemes are the colours of the six *Buddleja davidii* planted at intervals on the inside of the pergola. They include 'Empire Blue', 'Pink Beauty', 'White Cloud', 'Black Knight', 'Summer Beauty' and 'Purple Prince'.

Each section is colour-coordinated with its neighbouring section, so that although the sections are

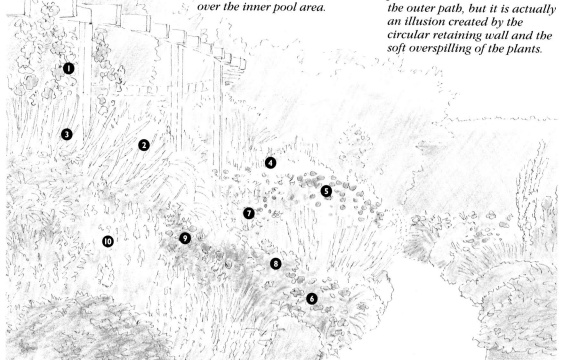

distinct, they also merge with each other. Plants in the outer sections are tall or medium-tall in height, so that as you curve along the circular path, outside the border, you can only see in to a certain level. Beyond the screen of plants is the rest of the border, but from the outside you can only guess at it, so retaining an element of surprise and interest in what is to come.

When you have criss-crossed the circular garden on the triangular paths, and walked the whole of the curved exterior path, there are numerous seats to find, as well as the sunken terrace at the garden's heart.

In this lower terrace there are some plants, mostly sun-loving Mediterranean varieties, grouped together in pots. The space in this area, the ability to look back at the border from an area without plants and the enjoyment of the small pool, make a tranquil garden. As you walk along the curved path, there is only one section of the border in view at any time, and you are always being invited to move on to view more, just around the corner.

Above: *As you walk along the curved outer path, only two borders are visible: the exterior one and the low- to medium-height plants of the outer section of the circular border. The taller plants at the foot of the pergola, and those that clothe the pergola itself, act as a screen to protect the privacy of the inner part of the garden.*

Vertical border

Altering the pace and focal effects of the border is usually achieved by using tall plants, set strategically into the scheme. If the border is backed by a wall, the range of plants available to add height is increased by climbing plants.

Clematis, roses, wisteria, ceanothus, honeysuckle, hop and passionflower are among the plants whose foliage and flowers, once the plants are established, will clothe the wall. Drapery of wisteria foliage and festoons of trailing flowers, the dinner-plate splashes of colour that large-flowered clematis offer, and the fragrance and colour of climbing roses, are just a few of the exterior decor attributes of climbing plants. Here it seems as if the vertical plane is just swirling out of the back of the border, to take your eye up the wall and across the arch, which the climbing plants frame so well.

Some, like ceanothus, do not support themselves and so support will have to be provided to keep them close to the wall.

In any case, a support system of vine eyes knocked into the masonry and wired up with green- or silver-coated wires, will be a bonus if you ever have to attend to the wall. Then it will be easier to remove the plants while work is in progress.

Plants growing up a wall are so much more visible than those just growing in the border, and therefore maintenance is important. For example, it is useful to keep a note of the type of clematis or rose, with times for cutting back. As they grow, tie in stems of clematis, rose and honeysuckle. In such a close planting, if they were left to themselves they are likely to tangle, with the result that both the flowers and the stems may get damaged.

New wisteria growth should be cut back and tied in summer, after flowering. Deadheading of roses keeps a succession of flowers going, but some plants, such as clematis, have attractive whirly seedheads, that come to prominence once the petals have fallen, and these offer an ornamental bonus.

If the border does not have a wall to back it, vertical effects can be achieved by growing annual climbing plants such as sweetpeas on a wall of canes and netting. It will take a few weeks in the growing season for them to get up to a good height, but with constant picking and

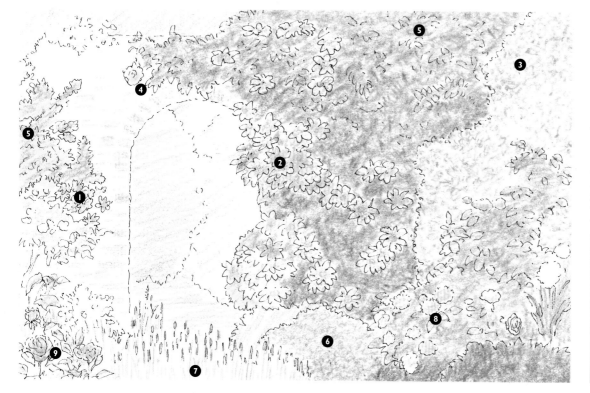

PLANT LIST	
1	*Clematis* 'H.F. Young'
2	*Clematis* 'Lawsoniana'
3	*Ceanothus americanus* 'Cascade'
4	*Rosa* 'Golden Shower'
5	*Wisteria sinensis*
6	*Hebe* 'Red Edge'
7	*Lavandula* 'Hidcote'
8	*Rosa* 'Mme Isaac Periere'
9	*Rosa* 'Gertrude Jekyll'

deadheading, a continuous succession of flowers will offer passing beauty.

More rampant climbers such as the golden hop can also be kept in check by growing them on tripods of canes, and winding in new growth every few days. Jasmine and roses can be grown on a more formal tripod in the border, and if there is space, a rope system is an attractive support for roses.

Above: *Ceanothus, clematis, roses, honeysuckle and wisteria each clothe the wall in their turn and add an element of height to the enclosed garden.*

Contained border

The border's edge is an important element of the overall look of the garden. In most gardens it is just an edge cut in the grass that surrounds the border. With a little extra thought, the edge can become an integral part of the planting plan.

Above: Iris *'Jane Phillips' and peonies are framed by the low-growing box hedge.*

PLANT LIST

1 *Buxus sempervirens* 'Suffruticosa'
2 *Iris* 'Jane Phillips'
3 *Paeonia* 'Sarah Bernhardt'
4 *Hosta* 'Blue Moon'

6 *Nepeta mussinii*
7 *Clematis* 'General Sikorski'
8 *Clematis* 'Acton Splendour'
9 *Lonicera periclymenum* 'Graham Thomas'

In formal and more grandiose gardens, sometimes the whole border or a particular garden area is enclosed or contained by a perfectly manicured wall of a green hedge, such as yew, holly or conifer. The enclosing effect of such a large boundary is to add a sense of walls and room space to the garden. The green walls contain the fragrance, provide a foil for the colour and make it easier to contain the visual experience as a whole.

On a smaller scale, a low-growing edging hedge can offer similar effects. The neatly-clipped box hedge around the herbaceous perennials in the border here acts as a restraint. It stops the plants flopping out over the path, like the sprawling

Nepeta mussini and *Stachys lanata* in the next border.

Box hedging at a slightly higher level is useful around a rose border to disguise the thorny legs of the roses, as well as to enclose and hold the floral effects. The earliest contained gardens were grown inside the intricate ribbon work of knot gardens. Low box edges framed the choice plants that early gardeners enjoyed, and held them for all to view. In a knot garden setting, the edging loses its plant look and becomes an architectural feature, more like a low wall of greenery, than a series of individual plants.

Box also envelopes the plants in the border, turning them into a well-wrapped bouquet of colour and fragrance. Its clean edge is an effective contrast to the fuller lines of the plants it contains. Although it needs close clipping in spring and late summer, it reduces the amount of cutting back and tidying up that you have to do with plants that spill onto paths.

Border plants such as *Lavandula* 'Hidcote', *Alchemilla mollis* and border pinks, can also be used to surround the border, although their effect during the summer flowering period will be less formal. Instead of a plant edging a path, or mowing edge of bricks, will be just as effective to contain the overspill from the border, and make mowing easier. Once again, the look will be less formal than that of a box edging, but the plants will make their own patterns and soften the bricks or pavers.

Right: *Here the "framed" plants contrast with the free-flowing plants on the left of the path.*

Giant plants

In most gardens space is too precious to allow it to be taken over by the giants of the plant world, but if there is space for them, large plants cover the ground well and provide dramatic effects.

Above: *Clouds of tiny flowers held high above the foliage are the attributes of* Crambe cordifolia. *Just as large, and considered dangerous since it may cause skin reactions, is the giant hogweed* Heracleum mantegazzianum.

Giant plants offer a sense of defiance and energy as they open from relatively small buds and rise to a huge stature. Half of the enjoyment is in watching this latent energy as they open and grow to fill more than their allotted space. The leaves of the giant plants suppress weeds and competition from self-seeders very effectively, lowering the maintenance of the border. A limited amount of time needs to be spent pruning some foliage out to allow others to succeed.

In this bog garden border filled with large plants, the drama of massive leaves and huge flower spikes seems almost primeval, as the foliage of *Gunnera manicata* unfurls to a majestic 2m (6ft) width on stems 3m (10ft) tall. Although this mighty plant with its rough, tough-toothed foliage and stems is frost hardy, its crown (all that is left in winter) needs protection from cold winds. You can do this by using its own spent leaves, piles of bracken or compost to cover the crown. In early summer, it carries a conical flowerhead, which is followed in autumn by orange seedpods, adding to the drama of its size.

Other giant plants that go well with this architectural plant are giant rhubarbs, with their differing foliage, *Rheum palmatum tanguticum* and *R. undulatum.* Similar to garden rhubarb, they grow to about 2m (6ft) and have a tall flower stem with a shower of small white flowers at the head in summer.

In a damp soil such as this, the umbrella plant *Darmera peltatum* with its wonderful sheltering foliage, will grow well. It carries its attractive flowers on tall bare stems that rise early in spring, straight out of the ground. Soon after the flower dies down the foliage begins to unfurl. Like the giant rhubarbs, it grows to 2m (6ft).

In a border like this, it is important to keep the large scale going and plant only giants, with a few very choice small plants at their feet to emphasize the size of the others. In this border in spring, that role falls to primulas of every sort, that spread at the leaf edges, as best they can.

Other tall-growing plants for these moist conditions include the giant form of Joe Pye weed, *Eupatorium purpureum.* With strong upright stems and a mass of small pink flowers on each flowerhead, it makes a stately show in late summer through to autumn. The giant form of meadowsweet, *Filipendula kamtschatica,* growing to 1.5m (5ft) with its attractive head of starry, scented white to pale pink flowers, is attractive in early summer. The large grass *Miscanthus sacchariflorus* or silver banner grass, with the silky-silver appearance of its flower spikes, makes a good specimen plant for the edge of a pond or stream, as well as in the bog garden. The large-leaved *Petasites japonicus giganteum* makes its presence felt in the border and as it is invasive, it

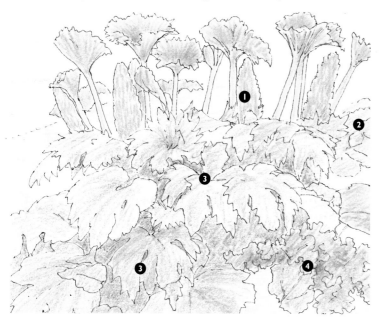

PLANT LIST

1 *Gunnera manicata*
2 *Petasites japonicus giganteum*
3 *Rheum undulatum*
4 *Rheum palmatum tanguticum*

needs to be dug out if it has spread where you do not want it.

There are a wide range of plants that grow on less moist soils that can make up a well-drained giant border. Among them is *Angelica gigas,* with its massive mauve-purple heads of flowers that unfurl over several weeks from their lemony-green buds. The giant brassica *Crambe cordifolia,* with its tough-looking foliage and tiny, delicate flowers carried as clouds high above the stems, is another giant for the high and mighty border.

Below: Like primeval figures in the mist, the foliage and flowerheads of Gunnera manicata *dominate the bog garden of giant plants. Two types of ornamental rhubarb,* Rheum palmatum tanguticum *and* R. undulatum *in the foreground make their own contrasting foliage display. To the right of the border the umbrella plant* Darmera peltatum *and the giant wintersweet* Petasites japonicus giganteum *fight it out with each other for supremacy.*

Rose border

Roses once used to be grown in separate borders devoted solely to their cultivation. In such a border, their summer glory could be admired, but after flowering, their thorny, bare stems and falling foliage in autumn looked unattractive.

Today in most domestic gardens the rose has come in from the cold and joined the party in the flower border with other plants. Old roses, in particular, need good herbaceous partners. Beautiful and fragrant they may be when in flower during high summer, but their season of beauty is short and soon they need the cluster of companions to disguise their own shortfalls.

However, while they are in flower there are so many herbaceous perennials, as well as annuals, that look attractive with them, that it is worthwhile choosing plants to complement and harmonize with the full fragrant blooms of the old roses. The range of plants that mix happily with roses is wide. Ground-covering, softly pastel-flowered geraniums such as

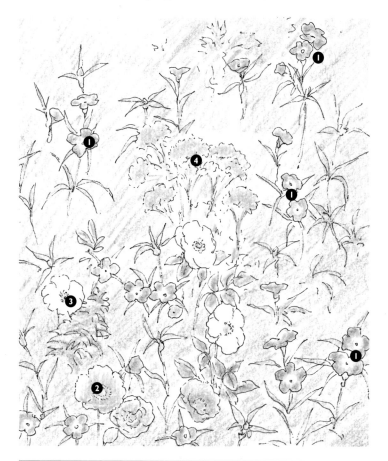

Above: *The soft full blooms of* Rosa 'Comte de Chambord' *are enhanced by the edging of upright, blue spikes of* Lavandula *'Hidcote'.*

PLANT LIST

1 Agrostemma githago
2 Papaver rhoeas 'Mother of Pearl'
3 Rosa 'Iceberg'
4 Thalictrum aquilegiifolium

Geranium endressii, Geranium pratense 'Mrs Kendal Clarke' and *Geranium phaeum* in its white or purple form, and *Alchemilla mollis* and primulas are good companions in season.

Tall spires of white or mauve foxgloves are the romantic's choice for a rose border, but for lower cover around the roses, the red, button-like flower of *Knautia macedonica* on long thin stems is attractive. Lamium with its streaky silver-leaved and pink-hooded flowers is good at ground level, while phlox in white or shades of pink and penstemon in pink, mauve and burgundy make a pleasing contribution at mid-height.

In this border, a romantic, painterly look has been created using delicately coloured annuals. The natural, simple flowers of corn cockle, *Agrostemma githago,* which grows to 1m (3ft) and carries its pastel flowers on will-o-the-wisp stalks, rise above the white blooms of *Rosa* 'Iceberg'. Taking up the same pastel shades, but with a metallic finish, are the delicate papery blooms of the poppy, *Papaver rhoeas* 'Mother of Pearl'. Taller perennials such as *Thalictrum aquilegiifolium,* with its silvery foliage and frothy flowers, rise even higher above the cultivated former cornfield flowers and roses. Hollyhocks, dame's violet and silene are also planted in the border and there

Right: *A painterly image is created by mixing corn cockle* Agrostemma githago *with the metallic poppies 'Mother of Pearl' and sowing them into the same border as delicately scented white* Rosa *'Iceberg'.*

are low-growing miniature roses to enjoy at a lower level in the mixed herbaceous border. Unlike old roses, the miniatures will flower over a long period, and some, depending on the species and type, offer small, often bronze-edged foliage.

Although the under- and inter-planting of roses with many other plants may make rose maintenance slightly more difficult, it is worthwhile for the longer flowering and the harmonious combinations which can be achieved. Spring bulbs, including crocus and snowdrops, and spring bedding such as aubrieta and violas will also suit the base of roses.

Roses will thrive if they can be mulched around their roots in spring, so avoid planting them too closely. If you need to spray during the growing season, avoid doing so on hot or windy days as you may damage the surrounding plants. Regular deadheading, and for old roses, cutting out of suckers and tying or shortening of whippy new growth, is necessary. Old roses also look attractive if their stems are arched and tied down to encourage more flower stems to break along the branch.

Grass border

With its flowing lines and gently shimmering movement, grass adds excitement to the border, whether it is planted with other grasses or mixed in with herbaceous plants.

Grasses offer a grace of line and form, variety of texture and seasonal colour, flowers and rippling movement. Their most attractive contribution is the way they can harmonize and contrast with other plants. They also provide a natural feel and with the wide range of heights, foliage colour and flower styles available, they can fit into most sites in a border.

In spring, the grass foliage is as its freshest and depending on the species makes attractive mounds or thin spiky accents. Once the grass flowers develop in late summer and autumn, the grass takes a central role. When strategically placed, leaves seem to catch fire in the autumn sun and delicate, straw-coloured flowers glisten in the back lighting of the sun. The gleaming effect of flowers and leaves is heightened by the rippling and rustling movements that any breath of wind creates

Above: *In a garden setting, large clumps of* Miscanthus sinensis *offer a strong architectural focus. In the sunlight its delicate flowers seem to shimmer, adding a sense of movement and rhythm to the planting.*

in foliage and flowers alike. The effect is almost the same as that of water shimmering and moving in the sun.

Some grasses such as dune grass, *Elymus magellanicus,* is invasive, but will grow well in a container to make a bluish accent with its blue-green foliage and beige flowers. If you do plant it in the ground, sink it in a bottomless bucket, as you might plant mint. The variegated ribbon grass or gardener's garters is also invasive, and should be avoided in a small garden, but if you have a large area to cover, its invasive nature will be welcome.

For the front of the border there is the mound-forming blue grass *Festuca glauca.* For ground

PLANT LIST
1 *Miscanthus floridulus*
2 *Calamagrostis* x *acutiflora* 'Stricta'
3 *Pennisetum villosum*

cover, choose *Festuca gautieri,* with its mounds of fresh green foliage and golden flowers on long silver stems, or *Carex plantaginea,* with its pleated, plantain-like leaves.

For a "see-through" screening effect, grow *Calamagrostis* x *acutiflora* 'Stricta'. Planted in some profusion here, it makes a bold statement with its straight brown flower spikes. Some of the taller grasses such as miscanthus and calamagrostis work well on their own as fillers. Their slim upright stems and strap-like leaves fill the gaps between neighbouring plants without detracting from them. They come into their own later in the season when their flowers and foliage shimmer in the sun. *Deschampsia caespitosa* has delicate flowers that glimmer and dance in the wind and the sun, but for the loveliest effects of movement, shape and texture, *Melica altissima* 'Atropurpurea' is first choice. Its flowers fall to one side like a small rain shower.

Below: *In this planting, only three grasses have been used and yet the effect is varied. At the back is* Miscanthus floridulus *or giant Chinese silver grass.*

This grows to 3m (10ft) and makes a silvery-metallic focal point if used in a small group. Here the effect is more striking. Calamagrostis x acutiflora *'Stricta' is in front of it, with upright stems that grow to 1.5m (5ft) and make a strong vertical accent. The effect is softened by the furry flowers of* Pennisetum villosum *in the foreground.*

Foliage border

Shape, colour, texture, architectural stature and delicate accents are just some of the ornamental offerings that plants grown more for their foliage than their flowers make to the border's beauty.

Sometimes the foliage effects come from plants that do not flower, or whose flowers are considered secondary, such as those of the plantain lily or hosta. In most cases, plants are chosen for a combination of their attributes, but those with good foliage earn their place in the border with great ease.

Evergreen foliage in its various colours and variegations makes up the permanent framework in the planting scheme. But plants such as ferns or hostas, whose fronds and leaves die down each year, offer an extra dimension. As they unfurl, the curving fronds or, in the case of hosta, rolled leaves, provide a sort of foretaste of their future size and texture. Later, when it is fully open and mature, hosta foliage makes an architectural impact. Ferns, so useful in shady, damp areas, offer a more delicate tracery.

Hostas are used here to make a bold, shapely block of colour and are available in a variety of leaf colours including golden, waxy-blue and variegated creamy white and green. They make a ruff-like edge to the border, shaping it and screening the feet of neighbouring plants.

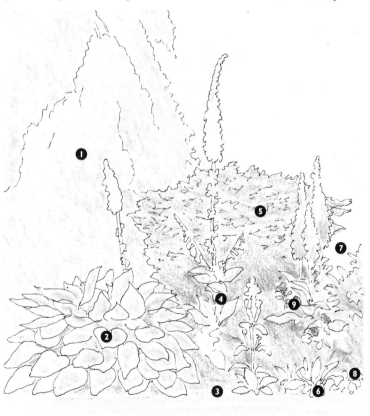

PLANT LIST

1 *Betula youngii*
2 *Hosta fortunei aureomarginata*
3 *Sedum maximum* 'Atropurpureum'
4 *Digitalis purpurea* 'Alba'
5 *Acer palmatum atropurpureum*
6 *Stachys lanata*
7 *Iris foetida*
8 *Heuchera* 'Pewter Moon'
9 *Geranium* 'Johnson's Blue'

Above: *Layer on layer of hosta foliage crowds the edge of the border, making a strong architectural impact through the growing season.*

Opposite: *Although there are flowering plants in this section of the border, the main impact comes from the colour and shapes of the plant foliage.*

Good foliage effects can be had from plants with coloured leaves. Purple foliage from the smoke bush, *Cotinus coggygria*, purple sage, dwarf berberis clipped into formal shapes and the deep purples of acers all offer excitement and good foliage accents to the border. Likewise, golden foliage provides colour and texture. Some golden-leaved plants such as golden marjoram need to be grown in shade to protect their foliage from sun scorch.

Midway between green and gold, the lemony-green, furry leaves of *Alchemilla mollis* have an extra delight. At each leaf's centre there is a small depression, and this holds drops of dew, like a little cup. Once this dew was thought to be the purest for washing the face.

In autumn, the real show-stoppers in the border come out in force. Acers, grasses and small trees and shrubs take on their seasonal colour before losing their leaves. In this border, the purple-leaved *Acer palmatum atropurpureum* becomes fiery red and if it is planted so that it is backlit with the low-setting sun, it becomes almost incandescent. Some forms of *Acer palmatum* turn gold, others orange or red. Hostas lose the chlorophyll in their leaves and become an attractive yellow.

In this border, the foliage of the hostas cools down the purple of the acer and makes a good contrast for the small leaves of the weeping birch whose shape and bark are such strong features in the border. In autumn, the yellow of the hosta and red of the acer fight it out in the fading sunlight, glowing when all the herbaceous perennials have been cut back.

Vegetable border

Flowers, foliage, shape, texture, architectural impact – and the bonus of productivity: these are the special border delights of vegetables.

For centuries, vegetables have been banished from the ornamental garden, to grow in isolation in kitchen gardens in regimental, but productive rows. But today, these kitchen gardens or potagers are as ornamentally interesting as any flower border. Their only drawback is that instead of maintaining the plants to the end of the growing season, they have to be harvested at the right moment. One of the most impressive ornamental kitchen gardens is at Villandry, France, where in autumn, ranks of ornamental cabbages in pink, white, and gray edge the beds of flowers and vegetables.

In the kitchen garden shown here, planned around two pear

trees that already grew in the garden, the central ornamental focus comes from the urn filled with nasturtiums and pelargoniums. The potager was designed to reduce the maintenance in a large garden, which had previously been grown rather like a vegetable allotment for two families.

The beds were planned to be large enough to grow a good crop in, and yet small enough to be managed from the surrounding paths. Each crop can be harvested fresh, or picked to freeze for later use. The beds can be individually maintained, sprayed or protected against weather or insect attack, and weeds are easy to hoe off or hand weed from any of the paths around the beds. The paths are wide enough to take wheelbarrows and to walk along easily. Each angular bed is edged with shuttering boards to keep the garden soil off the paths.

Although the brassicas here are grown for their use, the gray

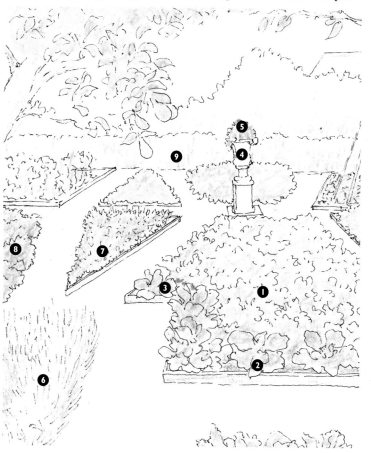

PLANT LIST

1 Cabbage F1 hybrid 'Julius'
2 Cabbage 'Spitfire'
3 Red salvia
4 Nasturtiums
5 Pelargoniums
6 Lavender
7 Carrots
8 Potatoes
9 Hedge of *Centaurea cyanus*

Opposite: *Sweet peas grown here on cane wigwams help to add height and floral interest to a bed of parsnips.*

Right: *In the large bed in the foreground two types of cabbage battle it out for space, while in the bed to the left, the feathery leaves of carrots make a delicate show. Red pelargoniums and nasturtiums fill the urn at the centre of the potager.*

foliage makes a handsome display throughout the growing season. It is combined with red salvias to provide a little dash of extra colour in summer. Potatoes, carrots, onions, gherkins, tomatoes and beans are among the vegetables that are regularly harvested from the potager. In autumn, the empty beds are dug over, manured and left over the winter. Some, though, are planted with winter vegetables, such as the hot and spicy Oriental vegetables protected with a layer of horticultural fleece.

In the ornamental vegetable garden, in general, there are strong colour effects to be achieved. Ruby chard, with red stems and red veining in leaves, is highly ornamental and eaten the same way as its relative the white-stemmed Swiss chard. There are purple Brussels sprouts, purple-coloured beans and peas. Red-leaved orach, an old-fashioned vegetable whose leaves are treated as spinach, is a showy plant to have in the middle of the border.

Parsley, lettuce and other salad herbs make suitable short-term edging for vegetable beds and a flowering herb, such as lavender, will attract bees and other insects for pollination.

Herb border

Herbs are usually grown in herb gardens where their ornamental beauty, as well as their culinary, medical and cosmetic uses, are much appreciated by herb enthusiasts. But their decorative charms also have a place in the informal flower border.

There are herbs for height, such as the feathery-leaved fennel, with its yellow umbrella-like flowerheads in summer that grows to about 1m (3ft). Lovage and angelica, too, offer good height, and they also provide architectural shapes, good for accents in the border. Cardoons, *Cynara carduculus,* with their silvery leaves, are more at home in the vegetable garden, but also look attractive in the border with old roses and white-flowered jasmine, grown for their herbal fragrance.

Sage in golden, purple or green leaf forms makes an attractive bushy shape for the front of the border, and if left to flower, produces headily aromatic flowers in white, pink or blue. Like lavender, it can be used to make an informal edge to a flowerbed. Clove pinks, traditionally grown in herb gardens for their fragrant flowers, are easy to use in the flower border, with their silver leaves making an additional contribution. Other useful and decorative herbs in the middle of a border are echinacea, or coneflower, a member of the daisy family and now much discussed for its possible medical uses; monarda or bergamot with its showy and colourful bracts, and marjoram, with its display of attractive foliage and flowers.

In this garden, the herbs have been used to create a loosely formal feature in the middle of a terrace hung with wall-supported plants. Golden marjoram is at the centre of the planting, with a box hedge to contain its glowing effects. Chives with their mauve flowers fill the triangular shapes at the edge of the plan and various thymes fill the rectangles beyond the main herb feature. Although segregated to a degree, the herbs as a whole combine well

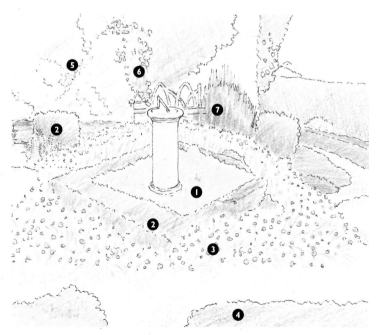

PLANT LIST

1 *Origanum vulgare* 'Aureum'
2 *Buxus*
3 *Allium schoenoprasum*
4 *Thymus sp*
5 *Fremontodendron californicum*
6 *Abutilon*
7 *Rosmarinus officinalis*

Above: *First planted in wedge-shaped segments, the herbs in this circular bed have developed their own informal patterns.*

Opposite: *The sunshine glow of golden marjoram lights up the centre of this herb feature on a flower-filled terrace.*

with the flowering plants that grow on the terrace. An abutilon and yellow Californian rose, *Fremontodendron californicum,* grow against the wall, and in one corner a bush of rosemary offers its aromatic foliage and later flowers to the scene.

Some herbs such as borage, comfrey, mint and costmary have attractive foliage and flowers, but their invasive nature means that you have to have space to allow them to spread.

They will make a good display in a rough site, where they will suppress all competing weeds.

Herbs such as chives and parsley make short-term but attractive edging for informal cottage garden borders, and the fragrant creeping thyme and chamomile are useful to make aromatic paths and seats in the garden. As you put pressure on them, the fragrance of their essential oils is released to perfume the air.

Half-hardy border

Some of the most attractive plants in the border have to be nurtured as cuttings over the winter or sown under glass to protect them from frosts. Known as half-hardy plants, their long-flowering displays make them worth the extra work.

Half-hardy annuals have to be sown each year in protected circumstances to prevent frosts killing them. Some half-hardy perennials, such as cannas, osteospermum and argyranthemum, can be over-wintered in a greenhouse or grown on from cuttings taken in autumn. Others, including osteospermum, will survive winter outdoors in mild areas, but as an insurance policy it is always best to have cuttings in the greenhouse.

Borders devoted to half-hardy plants come into their own from late spring onwards. Until then they look a little bare, but once the plants have got established and put on foliage and begin to flower, the colourful display seems never-ending.

Planted here in an island bed, the white *Osteospermum* 'Weetwood' spreads well to make a dense planting. Its foliage, green on top with a whitish-silver undersurface, is also attractive. This blends in with the small silver leaves of the mound-forming helichrysum that acts as a buffer between plants in this border. Beyond it is a pool of colour from a pink-flowered osteospermum. *Bidens ferulifolia*, a yellow-flowered favourite of bedding plans and hanging baskets, makes good ground cover and with its lemony flowers bridges the colour gap between the pinks and mauves of the osteospermums and the variegated leaves of *Canna malawiensis* 'Variegata'.

Canna foliage is attractive whether variegated, purple or plain green, but when in full flower, it reaches its maximum height, and becomes the focal point in a planting. This associates well with grasses, whose soft feathery flowers look attractive next to the canna's rather fleshy leaves. Here, the annual toadflax, or linaria, makes a good foil to the canna's solid foliage. Cannas should be treated like dahlias and lifted from the border once the first frosts have had their effect. The tubers should be cleaned and potted up into fresh soil, but kept dry and warm over winter. Then in spring, watering begins and once frost danger is over, they can be planted outside into the garden.

The half-hardy regime begins in early autumn when you should take cuttings from the plants you want to preserve. Put them five to a pot into a shaded greenhouse and cover them with polythene until the cuttings are rooted. In winter, the plants stay in the heated greenhouse and are kept just dry. In spring, they are removed from their communal pots and potted up singly and their growing tips pinched out to encourage them to become bushy. In late spring or early summer, the new plants go into their growing sites. Then they are watered in well and left to establish.

Opposite: *Half-hardy plants that flower from spring through to late summer need to be sown each year if they are annuals, or, if they are perennials, grown from cuttings or plants over-wintered in the greenhouse.*

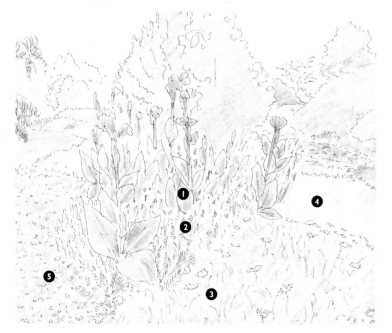

PLANT LIST
1 *Canna malawiensis* 'Variegata'
2 *Linaria*
3 *Osteospermum* 'Weetwood'
4 *Plechostachys serpyllifolia* (was *Helichrysum microphyllum*)
5 *Bidens ferulifolia*

Annual border

Bright and cheery annual flowers provide the quickest and easiest colour in a flower border, and they are useful as seasonal fillers in a perennial border.

Annual is the term used to describe plants that are sown every year and that grow, flower and set seed all in the same year. There are many annuals to choose from to achieve a colourful, but seasonal, display in the garden. Some can be sown directly into their growing sites, while others, known as half-hardy annuals, need cosseting with warmth and protection before they are planted out into the warm soil in spring. If you want to, you can sow hardy annuals into trays in a greenhouse to plant out when the soil warms up again, but unless you have both the time and the resources, this is not necessary.

Instead, rake the already prepared soil in the border until there is a fine tilth. Then decide where you want different blocks of colour, and of course, bear in mind the varying heights and spaces that should be allocated to different plants. Use a cane to mark out various shapes in the soil. These will then be the sites for sowing. Within each block, mark out parallel lines or drills along which you will sow the seed. Most annual seed should be sown to a depth of 5-15mm (¼-½in) and in rows that are evenly spaced to 20-30cm (8-12in) apart.

Sowing into neat rows in blocks means that in a few weeks time, when the seed has germinated, it will be instantly recognizable and stand out from any annual weed seeds that will have germinated as well. It will be easy to hand weed at this stage and also to thin out seedlings from overcrowded rows. Leave space in the planting scheme to allow for the half-hardy annuals that you have sown in the greenhouse, and when the plants are large enough, plant them out into their growing site.

Watering is necessary while the plants become established, particularly in dry seasons, but beyond that, the only maintenance is to deadhead and tidy up the plants as they grow. The more you deadhead the plant, the more flowering is encouraged. During the summer it will give the plants an extra boost if you give them liquid feed when you water. At the end of the flowering season leave some flowers to develop seeds and then some of your work next year will be done for you, when the self-sown seedlings germinate in spring.

The range of plants and

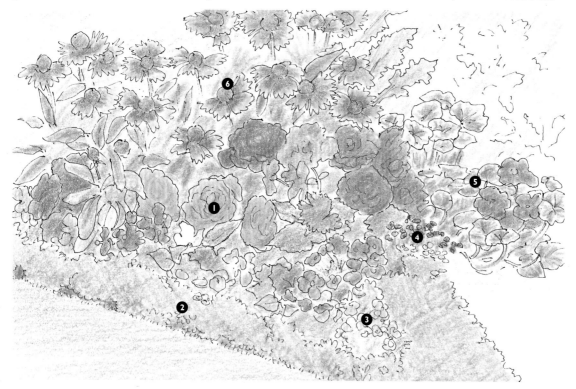

PLANT LIST

1 *Begonia* 'Non-Stop Mixed' hybrids
2 *Matricaria* 'Santana Lemon'
3 *Begonia* 'Burgundy'
4 *Lobelia erinus compacta* 'Blue Wings'
5 *Nasturtium tropaeolum* 'Alaska'
6 *Gaillardia* hybrids

colours that are available is wide, and the seed companies are always extending their lists with new and better seed strains. Some offer colour-coordinated selections with a range of heights, so that you can achieve a harmonious effect just by sowing into different parts of the border.

Below: *In this vibrant border, hardy and half-hardy annuals are used in combination with the perennial blanket flower,* Gaillardia *hybrids. At the edge, the half-hardy annual,* Matricaria *'Santana Lemon' is growing as a low frame. The half-hardy annual* Begonia *'Non-Stop Mixed' rises above the* smaller-flowered, fibrous-rooted *half-hardy* Begonia *'Burgundy'. Half-hardy* Lobelia erinus compacta *'Blue Wings' and hardy annual* Nasturtium tropaeolum *'Alaska' tumble over the paving and the bright display is backed by a group of perennial blanket flowers,* Gaillardia *hybrids.*

Child's border

Bright colours, quick results and fun are the three main elements that are needed in a garden area for a child to enjoy.

Above: *The dwarf sunflower* Helianthus annuum *'Smile Baby' lines the path.*

PLANT LIST

1 *Centaurea cyanus* 'Midget Mixed'
2 Strawberry 'Sweetheart'
3 Onion 'Red Mate'
4 *Iberis umbellata*
5 Cucumber 'Sweet Slice'
6 *Helianthus annuum* 'Mammoth'
7 *Helianthus annuum* 'Autumn Beauty'
8 *Tanacetum parthenium* 'Aureum'
9 *Helianthus annuum* 'Teddy Bear'
10 Ruby chard
11 Pumpkin 'Spooky'
12 Strawberries
13 Potato
14 Tomato 'Little Pear'
15 *Tagetes* 'Lemon Gem'
16 *Osteospermum* 'High Noon'
17 Heartsease

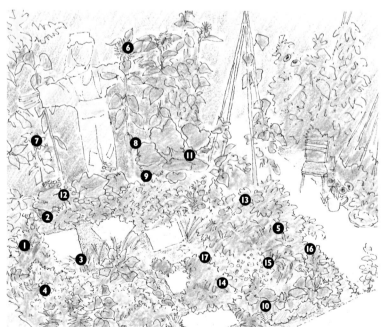

Long ago sunflowers, *Helianthus annuum*, were just tall and had one huge flower face to a stem. Now they come in all heights, many colours and with several flowers to each stem. They are good fun to grow and provide height and colour fairly quickly. For extra fun, let individual family members sow their own sunflower patch, and race the others for height supremacy or for first past the flowering post. For productivity, lettuces and radishes are usually the swiftest off the mark and the range of colourful and shapely lettuces available, will provide an ornamental bonus.

In this garden, rat's tail radish, grown for its seedpod rather than its root, provided early white flowers on unruly plants in spring. By mid-summer, the pods were ready to pick and, since they were too hot for children to relish, were offered to parents to eat in stir-fried dishes or to pickle for later use.

French and African marigolds, the lemon-coloured *Tagetes* 'Lemon Gem' and a sunny orange osteospermum make a bright display and attract insects needed to pollinate the tomatoes and climbing beans. On the other side of the border, a more subdued but delightful and floriferous row of dwarf mixed colour cornflowers joins with strawberries. Within the bed and among the stepping stones are heartsease, flame nettle and strawflowers – all favourites with children, but best bought as bedding plants or sown by green-fingered adults.

Also in the productive part of the garden is ruby chard, not known for its popularity with children as an edible plant, but rather for its colourful leaves and stems which provide a fun element in the garden. Cucumber 'Sweet Slice', a stray potato left in from last year and the shapely leaves of a halloween pumpkin, 'Spooky', will please children, and may even earn some pocket money if they are sold to consumers in the family or to neighbours.

Informal elements like the terracotta chicken complete with

a downy covering of golden thyme, the stylish scarecrow and a former parsley pig, now sporting a succulent plant, Echevaria, add interest.

Sunflowers, pumpkin, lettuce and ruby chard can be sown straight into the ground in late spring, as can the annuals such as the dwarf cornflowers and marigolds. Through the summer the garden needs weeding, deadheading and, hopefully, harvesting as flowers and vegetables come to maturity.

Below: *Scarecrow and sunflowers see eye-to-eye at the back of the mixed flower and vegetable border.*

Mobile border

Most borders grow in the ground and are permanently sited, even if the plants within them change from year to year or over the years. But even without a garden it is possible to have a border in containers.

Most people think of containers on patios and balconies, resplendent with summer bedding and annual flowers, but a mobile border can have some unusual perennials and even shrubs and trees. With the same sort of design and planning skills that border-making demands of gardeners, a stylish and ever-changing mobile garden can be achieved to suit the available space.

This garden, created for a sculptor to display his figures, sits on a gravel base and most of the pots are terracotta or glazed stoneware. Because the plants are in an artificial environment all their needs have to be supplied by the gardener. In this case, they are all potted in a loam-based compost with a good drainage layer and liquid seaweed fertilizer is applied regularly during the growing season. In spring, compost is forked into the larger pots and worked into the smaller ones with a handfork. The plants are repotted every few years, as they need it, so that they do not become root-bound and any that eventually outgrow their contained situation are retired into the main garden to continue their growth.

Regular watering is the most time-consuming part of the maintenance of a large collection of plants that can make up a mobile border. To lessen the work, an automatic drip system has been put in place, winding through the planting. Its pipes and sprinklers are hidden from view by the lush foliage of the plants they serve.

In spring, as ferns and grasses unfurl and before the climbing plants and bamboos put on their new leaves, the container border looks a little bare, but by the early summer the foliage is lush and it is sometimes easy to forget that the plants are growing in pots, as their growth is so good and strong. This particular mobile garden moves frequently as it has to act as a foil for the sculptures at shows. Its composition is transitory and if one grouping is unsuccessful, it can easily be changed.

Edged with York stone slabs and interspersed with salt-glazed Victorian chimney pots for extra focal effect, the mobile border boasts some large specimens of *Berberis atropurpurea* and a stand of bamboos, 2.7m (9ft) high. Foliage, shape and texture are the basis on which most of the plants are chosen. *Phormium tenax* 'Bronze Baby' with its metallic strap-like leaves and the golden hop, *Humulus lupulus* 'Aureus' and grasses, such as *Stipa gigantea* are among the foliage in containers.

PLANT LIST

1 Miniature bullrush
2 *Clematis macropetala*
3 *Anthemis cupaniana*
4 *Humulus lupulus* 'Aureus'
5 *Sedum morganianum*
6 *Allium caeruleum*
7 *Saxifrage*
8 *Juniperus virginiana* 'Grey Owl'
9 *Tylecodon reticulata*
10 *Osmunda regalis*
11 *Hebe*
12 *Dicentra formosa*
13 *Anemone japonica* 'Honorine Jobert'
14 *Stipa gigantea*
15 *Euphorbia wulfenii*
16 *Phormium tenax* 'Bronze Baby'

Left: *In the courtyard where the mobile border is based, there are a number of climbers already in place against the walls of the house and outbuildings, and these add to the illusion that the border is a permanent feature. On first sight, only the pots in the first row and the barrels for water plants are visible, so that it is hard to see where containers and permanent plants start and finish.*

Romantic border

Soft colours, fragrance, walls draped with swags of abundant blooms and beds filled with all the choicest of summer-flowering roses, peonies and iris are just some of the pointers to an informal and romantic style.

Although formal in their individual shapes, the character of the borders in this small walled garden is one of soft, romantic informality. Nearly all the wall space surrounding the borders is covered with climbers or wall plants such as *Ceanothus* 'Cascade', the white-flowered potato climber *Solanum jasminoides* and numerous clematis, all softening the texture of the hard landscaping. The impression is of a wall hung with generously draped, floral-printed textiles. The plants in each of the beds echo the colours of the 'wall hangings'

becoming more like soft furnishings than plants.

In spring, the box-edged beds are filled with single colour tulips, pink double early flowering *Tulipa* 'Angelique' and *Tulipa* 'White Triumphator', as well as Barnhaven primulas and numerous irises including 'Jane Phillips', 'Black Hills' and 'Braithwaite'. In early summer, peonies, including 'Duchesse de Nemours', 'Mrs Perry' and 'Cedric Morris', and roses come to the fore. Lavender takes the floral fragrance forward until the lilies, including 'Journey's End' and 'Sans Souci', open their

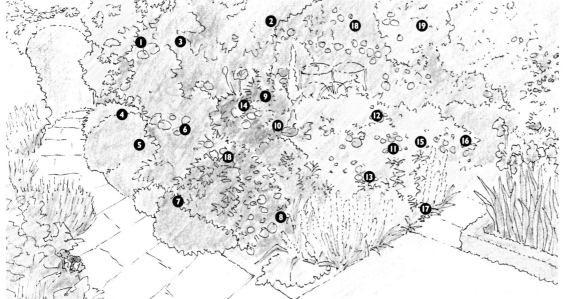

PLANT LIST

1 *Clematis henryii*
2 *Ceanothus* 'Cascade'
3 *Abelia grandiflora*
4 *Senecio* 'White Diamond'
5 *Hebe* 'Red Edge'
6 *Rosa* 'Gertrude Jekyll'
7 *Lavendula* 'Hidcote'
8 *Rosa* 'Queen of Denmark'
9 *Papaver orientale* 'Mrs Perry'
10 *Papaver* 'Cedric Morris'
12 *Rosa* 'Magenta'
12 *Buddleja* 'Nanho Blue'
13 *Artemisia ludoviciana*
14 *Juniperus scopulorum* 'Skyrocket'
15 *Rosa* 'Reine Victoire'
16 *Rosa* 'Heritage'
17 *Sisyrinchium striatum*
18 *Rosa* 'Constance Spry'
19 *Rosa* 'Mme Albert Carrière'

sumptuous blooms to overwhelm with their beauty and fragrance.

The softness of the blooms and shapes of the old roses within the beds is contrasted with the tall upright flower spikes of foxgloves in white and purple, and the creamy yellow of *Sisyrinchium striatum*. The contrasting nature of the soft foliage of roses and lavender, and the spiky foliage of sisyrinchium, as well as the iris, keep the style from becoming too sentimental. Similarly, anchoring the generous nature of the blooms in each of the beds, are plants with silver foliage. These plants are highly textured and they add to the already heady romance of the style, with their metallic colouring offering a glint of something rather more steely.

In keeping with the feel of the plants, the lion fountain and the white-painted wrought-iron bench offer the garden visitor a view into a less hurried and more indulgent world. On the surface, such a style looks easy to maintain, but behind the relaxed exterior there is a routine of regular maintenance.

In autumn, once plants die down they are cut back and tidied and manure is dug in around the plants, especially the roses. Old roses are cut back if their new growth is spindly, and lavenders are trimmed back, as are the box hedges. Clematis, depending on their flowering time, are cut back in autumn and spring and all climbing plants are tied in as they grow during the spring and summer.

Opposite: *The weathered statue of Flora is well-placed among sumptuous blooms of clematis, roses and geraniums.*

Below: *Evoking the essence of romance, of long summer nights and days. Fragrant roses, wall plants and pastel-coloured perennials combine well to make a very particular garden style.*

Meditation border

Depending on the mixture of plants and style, borders have varying effects on our senses. Some combinations of plants excite and stimulate, while others offer peace and tranquility – such as this border, created to be a place of meditation.

To create the right ambience for quiet repose only a few plants are necessary. Their large-scale planting does not allow for the visual or mental stimulation in the same way that a vibrant and floriferous border does and it allows the mind to be free, as is the eye, to roam back and forth along the edges of the paths, and there is plenty of space for thoughts and stillness.

This tranquil garden room is framed by high evergreen hedges of yew, *Taxus baccata,* on two sides and the conifer, *Thuja plicata* on one side (the fourth side is a wall of Kentish ragstone bricks or old Kent reds). The aim is to play down the senses and the energy that borders normally offer. Entering the garden is like coming upon a quiet, cloistered green room, set apart from the rest of the world. Even the seat, which is stonework from an old churchyard, contributes to the feeling of other worldliness.

The linear shapes of the paths and beds also contribute to the peaceful nature of the border. The tranquil planting is achieved by using *Alchemilla mollis* to line the border and to spill out onto the paths. Inside the lady's mantle edging are masses of Irish ivy, *Hedera helix* 'Hibernica'. The glossy leaves of the ivy contrast well with the soft and furry texture of the alchemilla leaves. The ivy is planted at a density of 30 plants per side and they took nearly three years to cover the ground allotted to them. Once or twice a year, they attempt to over-reach the space, and that is the time when they are cut back with a sharp spade.

The alchemilla was planted at a similar density and it is prevented from flopping over the path by a support of 35cm (15in) canes and garden twine. The flowers are cut off, which is a back-breaking exercise, in mid-July and new mounds of green leaves form. Although the alchemilla flowers offer a lime-yellow colour, it is the calm green ivy foliage that predominates in this garden.

In the two box-edged rectangles at the end of the meditation garden, *Viola cornuta* is used as a ground cover and, when they are better established, the two variegated box plants in the centre are to be trained as topiary columns.

In the late evening when the low-angled sun is setting, its rays light up the axis of the paths right up to the stone seat, giving the impression that it is more altar than seat. In the early morning too, the meditation garden has its special effects as the dew, held in the cupped foliage of *Alchemilla mollis,* dances with light.

PLANT LIST
1 *Alchemilla mollis*
2 *Hedera helix* 'Hibernica'
3 *Buxus sempervirens*
4 *Viola cornuta*

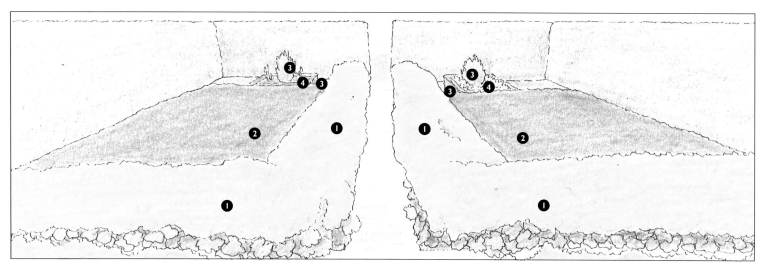

Right: *A simple plan of light and dark green plants, massed together, provided the inspiration for the meditation garden below.*

Below: *With no vibrant colours nor any dramatic changes in tempo or focus, the massed alchemilla and ivy plants allow for a calming of the senses and provide the precious time for quiet reflection.*

Cottage border

Certain plants, and the way in which they are combined, are reminiscent of a pastoral and romantic lifestyle in cosy, rose-clad cottages. This cottage gardening style evokes a sense of nostalgia for a time gone by.

It may look effortless to achieve, but a cottage garden border is the result of a constant round of activity that begins with the preparation of the soil in the autumn or early spring. In this hedge-enclosed cottage garden, cut by numerous straight paths, the chosen plants are a broad mixture of fairly common ones such as *Alchemilla mollis,* dianthus, *Lychnis coronaria* and

herbs including lavender, thyme and marjoram. They are supplemented by some rather more choice plants that fit well into the cottage garden theme, and at the same time have acquired a modern popularity. They include the South African daisy, *Osteospermum jucundum* and *Penstemon* 'Andenken an Friedrich Hahn'.

The roses are trained on metal

frames. The aim is to keep the old and shrub roses compact in the small area that they have to grow in, within the densely packed beds. They keep a good shape and offer a bowler hat of flowers at roughly the central part of the beds.

The skill in a cottage garden is to keep a succession of colour going from late spring right through to autumn, without

obviously replanting or replacing plants that end their flowering. In autumn, michaelmas daises, penstemon and *Dendranthema rubellum* take the show on. *Nicotiana* species and dame's violet, *Hesperis matronalis*, are added to provide fragrance, particularly in the evening, when the small terrace in the garden is an inviting place to sit. The fragrance and aroma of herbs

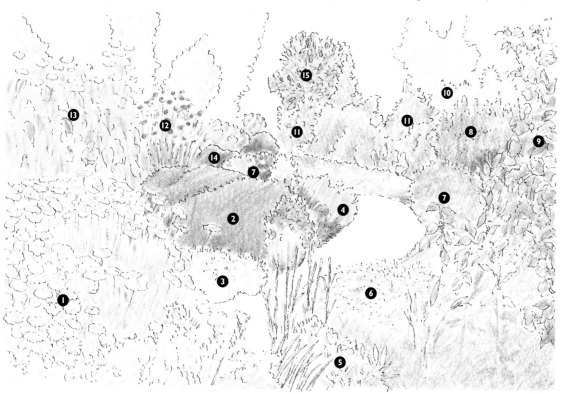

PLANT LIST

1 *Osteospermum jucundum*
2 *Ruta graveolens* 'Jackman's Blue'
3 *Thymus x citriodorus* 'Silver Queen'
4 *Origanum vulgare* 'Aureum'
5 *Artemisia ludoviciana* 'Silver Queen'
6 *Sedum spathulifolium*
7 *Dianthus sp.*
8 *Penstemon* 'Andenken an Friedrich Hahn'
9 *Rosa* 'Fantin-Latour'
10 *Rosa cantabrigiensis*
11 *Campanula persicifolia*
12 *Lychnis coronaria*
13 *Phlomis russeliana*
14 *Alchemilla mollis*
15 *Photinia x fraseri* 'Red Robin'

and flowers is enhanced by the green walls of hedges which seem to hold the fragrance as if in a pomander.

The cottage garden is in a dry situation on light, free-draining soil and needs regular watering, usually in the evening with a sprinkler. Tall plants such as echinops and thalictrum need staking. Deadheading continues through the season, but some plants are allowed to self-seed, and their seedheads are admired for the incidental ornament they offer. Apart from planting to fill gaps during the season, lifting and splitting clumps in autumn, mulching is one of the most important activities in the garden. All the material that is cut from the plants is chopped into smaller pieces and placed on the soil as an eco-mulch, saving energy in shredding it or otherwise disposing of it.

Below: *Soft mounds of colour from golden marjoram and silvery artemisia are among the delights of the plant-rich cottage garden.*

Penstemons

Borders where a single type of flower or plant dominates can hold as much interest as varied combinations. Popular in the Victorian garden, penstemons have had a recent revival and they are almost obligatory in modern borders.

Although penstemons look attractive mixed with other plants of similar shades within a border, a planting where several different varieties are grouped together makes a very satisfying way to display these stylish and floriferous plants. They flower over a long period from late June right through until November, so a border devoted solely to penstemons will repay its keep.

To get a good penstemon bed going, propagate annually from existing plants in autumn. Planted out in April, the new plants will take a year to establish. They will flower in the first year, but the flowers will be on smaller plants than when mature. The following spring, cut the tops of the plants and each will make many new stems and form a bushy, denser plant. In subsequent years this will increase until after two or three years the plants will begin to lose their vigour and flowering will be gappy. The process has to be started again.

Each spring, cut the plants back to encourage the formation of new shoots. Avoid doing this in autumn, as the old stems will provide shelter from frost and wind for the crown of the plant. Penstemons have a wide colour range and as they are dense and bushy, they do not need staking. Plant them 45cm (18in) apart to give them space to bush out.

PLANT LIST

1 *Penstemon* 'Pink Bedder'
2 *Penstemon* 'Blackbird'
3 *Penstemon* 'Cherry Ripe'
4 *Lavandula* 'Hidcote'
5 *Crocosmea* 'Lucifer'

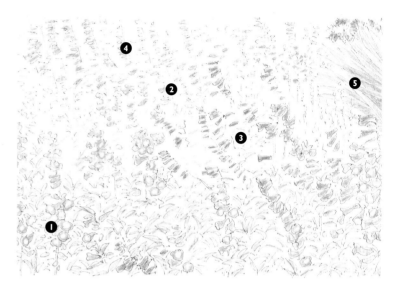

Below: *Colour from a single subject bed of penstemons begins in late June and continues right through to November.*

Sunflowers

Large-faced sunflowers make a jolly contribution to any border. There are so many different strains of sunflower seed available now that it is possible to devote a whole border to these bright annuals for maximum impact.

Below: *Just one variety of sunflower is visible in this small front garden, but the effect of the large bright flowers and lush leaves is eye-catching.*

As hardy annuals, sunflowers need no special attention to germinate them, and it is best to sow them "in situ" in early spring. Sow them into well-prepared, rich and moist ground. The seeds are large so it is simple to space them evenly along the border. For the back of the planting, the tallest variety is the common sunflower *Helianthus annuus*. At the front of the border there is a new dwarf sunflower, specially bred for small gardens and a particular favourite with children. Called 'Teddy Bear', its flowers are 15cm (6in) in diameter and it grows to 45cm (18in) high with several double flowers to each plant. Also small is 'Big Smile' which at 45cm (18in) tall has a broad golden face with a coal black central boss and looks good in a border or planted in containers.

Other tall-growing sunflowers include 'Italian White', which grows to 1.2m (4ft) and has a creamy white bloom with a golden and black central boss; 'Moonwalker' with seveal lemon-yellow flowers to each plant and growing to 2m (6ft) and 'Autumn Baby' with russet, yellow and chestnut coloured flowers. This is also tall, growing to 2m (6ft). 'Sunbeam', which has a lemon-yellow face and is almost pollen-free, is useful as a cut flower and it grows to a height of 1.2m (4ft).

Grasses

With a variety of colourful and shapely grasses now available, dramatic effects can be achieved.

In autumn as you drive along narrow country lanes or on busy motorways, you will notice that the roads are lined by a common vergeside plant, namely grass. It is at this time of the year, when the grasses are in flower and slightly bleached out by the summer sun, that they become more noticeable as a feature in the landscape. Their uniformity of line and the mass in which they are growing is attractive, and it catches your eye to take you round the next corner.

Similarly, grass can be used in a garden to make a simple but effective display that relies on its natural landscape attributes and makes them work in a border. If they are treated as large shrubs, they can be combined with other perennials and shrubs. They can also be planted as single subject groups, such as in this setting, where it will be easier to treat them as garden plants.

The tall, stately feather reed grass, *Calamagrostis* x *acutiflora* 'Stricta', is one of the most floriferous of perennial grasses, with its yellow flower spikes starting in June and continuing to look attractive through the winter months. Its flowers stand aloft on upright stems up to 1.5m (5ft) tall and appear to float in every breath of wind. Later in the season, the flower colour deepens to a bright gold. In this border where they are mass planted, the dense green stems make a strong background for the bird sculpture while at the same time contrasting very well with the beige flowers.

Left: Calamagrostis x acutiflora *'Stricta' makes a strong vertical line in the border and acts here as a frame and background for the naturalistic sculpture.*

Tulips

In these two borders, it is the tulips that dominate even though there are many other plants with them in each setting.

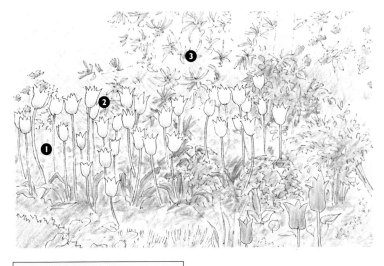

PLANT LIST
1 *Brunnera macrophylla*
2 *Tulipa* 'White Triumphator'
3 *Pyrus salicifolia* 'Pendula'

Below: *In spring, the lily-flowered* Tulipa *'White Triumphator' glistens against the blue of the forget-me-not and the silver of the weeping pear.*

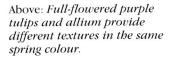

Above: *Full-flowered purple tulips and allium provide different textures in the same spring colour.*

In the above border, the full, wavy-edged *Tulipa* 'Blue Parrot' is not alone. But the density of the planting attracts the eye most emphatically and it is only later that you realize there are globes of the similarly purple allium, *Allium aflatunense,* rising just a little higher than the tulips.

In the second border (right), *Tulipa* 'White Triumphator', planted to a depth of 20cm (8in) in a hot and dry soil, continues to flower each year. Backed by the silver foliage of *Pyrus salicifolia* 'Pendula', the white of the tulips seems to shine with an almost metallic finish. The underplanting of *Brunnera macrophylla,* with its bright blue forget-me-not flowers, intensifies the sparkle of the tulip display.

PLANT LISTS

PLANTS FOR CLAY SOIL

Acanthus spp
Ajuga
Alchemilla mollis
Aquilegia
Aruncus dioicus
Astilbe
Bergenia
Brunnera
Campanula
Dicentra
Epimedium

ERIGERON 'PROSPERITY'

Erigeron
Geranium endressi
Hedera
Helenium
Helleborus
Hemerocallis
Hosta
Inula
Lamium
Ligularia
Lysimachia
Peltiphyllum
Persicaria
Petasites
Phlox paniculata (if soil has compost added and drainage is improved)
Phormium

SOLIDAGO 'GOLDEN MOSA'

Physostegia
Rodgersia
Rosa
Rubus
Rudbeckia fulgida
Solidago
Symphoricarpus
Trollius
Vinca

PLANTS FOR ACID SOIL

Arbutus
Azalea
Calluna
Camellia
Cornus
Corylopsis
Erica
Fothergilla
Lithodora diffusa 'Heavenly Blue'
Meconopsis grandis
Rhododendron

RHODODENDRON 'VINTAGE ROSE'

Smilacina racemosa
Trillium
Uvularia

PLANTS FOR CHALK AND LIMESTONE

Acaena
Acanthus
Achillea
Ajuga
Alyssum saxatile
Anaphalis
Anchusa
Aucuba
Berberis
Campanula
Centaurea

Choisya
Convolvulus
Crambe
Dianthus
Digitalis

DIGITALIS

Doronicum
Echinops
Epimedium
Euphorbia
Gaillardia
Galega
Hebe
Inula
Iris
Lavandula

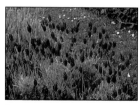

LAVANDULA STOECHAS

Linum
Liriope
Matthiola
Nemesia
Nepeta
Phlomis
Primula
Rosmarinus
Salvia
Santolina
Scabiosa
Sedum

Stachys
Tellima
Thymus
Viola
Zinnia

PLANTS FOR HOT SITES, DRY SANDY SOIL

Acanthus
Achillea

ACHILLEA FILIPENDULINA 'GOLD PLATE'

Alstroemeria
Alyssum
Anthemis
Armeria
Aubrietia
Bergenia
Buddleja
Caryopteris clandonensis 'Heavenly Blue'
Catananche
Cistus

CISTUS ALBIDUS

Coreopsis
Crambe
Cytisus
Dianthus
Erigeron
Euphorbia myrsinites

Festuca glauca
Genista
Geranium
Hebe
Helianthemum

HELIANTHEMUM 'HENFIELD BRILLIANT'

Kniphofia 'Little Maid'
Lavandula
Limonium
Macleaya
Miscanthus sinensis 'Silberspinne'
Nepeta
Oenethera
Papaver
Phlomis fruticosa
Romneya coulteri
Rosmarinus
Salvia
Santolina
Scabiosa
Sedum 'Ruby Glow'
Sedum x spectabile 'Brilliant'
Sedum telephium 'Atropurpureum'
Senecio
Silene
Stipa tenuissima
Thymus
Tulbaghia violacea
Verbascum
Veronica
Viola

TALL OR ARCHITECTURAL PLANTS

Acanthus
Angelica gigas
Crambe cordifolia

ACANTHUS MOLLIS

Darmera peltata
Echinops
Eupatorium cannabinum
Filipendulina kamtschatica
Gunnera manicata

GUNNERA MANICATA

Helianthus
Ligularia
Macleaya
Miscanthus saccharifolius
Onopordium acanthium
Phormium tenax
Rheum
Rodgersia
Silybum marianum
Verbascum
Vitis coignetiae

FOLIAGE PLANTS

Acaena
Acanthus
Acer
Artemisia
Arum italicum 'Pictum'
Carex morrowii 'Evergold'

ACER PALMATUM

Clematis integrifolia
Epimedium
Euonymus
Euphorbia sikkimensis
Festuca
Gunnera
Hakonechloa macra
  'Aureola'
Hedera
Helleborus
Heuchera
Humulus lupulus 'Aureus'

HUMULUS LUPULUS 'AUREUS'

Lamium
Ligularia
Lysichitum
Melianthus major
Milium effusum 'Bowles
  Gold'
Phormium
Pulmonaria
Rheum palmatum
Rodgersia
Rosa glauca
Rosa pimpinellifolia
Veratrum

PLANTS FOR MOIST SOILS

Ajuga
Arum italicum
Astilbe

Colchicum autumnale
Cornus alba

CORNUS ALBA 'SIBIRICA'

Cornus stolonifera
Geranium macrorrhizum
  'Album'
Geranium magnificum
Geranium pratense 'Flore
  Pleno'
Gunnera
Helleborus sternii hybrids
Ligularia
Lysichitum
Matteuccia
Milium effusum 'Bowles
  Gold'
Myosotis
Petasites japonicus
Trollius

TROLLIUS EUROPAEUS

PLANTS FOR DRY SHADE

Ajuga reptans
Alchemilla conjuncta
Alchemilla mollis
Aucuba
Bergenia cordifolia
Camellia

Carex
Cyclamen

CYCLAMEN COUM

Epimedium
Euphorbia robbiae
Geranium phaeum
Hedera
Iris foetidissima
Lamium maculatum

LAMIUM MACULATUM

Liriope muscari
Lunaria
Luzula
Mahonia
Myrrhis odorata
Thalictrum
Vinca minor

PLANTS FOR WOODLAND
SHADE UNDER TREES

Anemone
Asarum

ANEMONE HYBRIDA

Brunnera
Convallaria
Dicentra
Euonymus
Geranium macrorrhizum
Hebe
Hedera
Helleborus
Hosta
Hydrangea
Lysimachia
Pachysandra
Pulmonaria
Saxifraga
Tellima
Tolmeia
Viola

PLANTS FOR MOIST SHADE

Akebia quinata
Anemone x hybrida
  cultivars
Aruncus dioicus
Asplenium scolopendrium
Digitalis mertonensis
Euphorbia polychroma
Hacquetia epipactis
Hepatica nobilis
Hosta
Humulus lupulus 'Aureus'
Primula

PRIMULA JAPONICA

Rodgersia pinnata
Sanguinaria canadensis
Smilacina racemosa
Tiarella cordifolia
Tricyrtis fomosana
Trillium grandiflora
Uvularia grandiflora

PICTURE ACKNOWLEDGEMENTS

The Publisher gratefully acknowledge the following photography libraries for pictures used in this book.

Garden Picture Library: 28 (Howard Rice), 29 (Brigitte Thomas), 43 (David England). Jerry Harpur Picture Library: 1, 2, 3, 5, 22, 33, 35, 38, 39, 41, 45 (top and bottom), 46, 51, 59, 60, 61, 62, 64, 66, 67, 68, 77, 89, 90, 91 (bottom). Peter McHoy: 7, 8, 9, 10, 13, 18, 92 (all), 93 (all). Derek St Romaine: 27 (top and bottom), 30, 36, 37, 47, 48, 49, 55, 63, 65, 69, 70, 71, 73, 75, 78, 79, 81, 82, 83, 84 (bottom). Barbara Segall: 72. David Way: 23, 31, 50, 53, 56 (left and right), 57, 85 (top), 87, 88, 91 (top).

The scarecrow in the Child's border was kindly lent by Pamela Westland and was made by Polly Kettle, "The Maker of Scarecrows", Oakland Cottage, Greenway Lane, Charlton Kings, Cheltenham, Gloucestershire, GL52 6LA. Tel: 01242 239071

BORDERS FEATURED IN THE BOOK

The Publishers would like to thank the following owners for permission to include their gardens in the book.

Drs and Mevr. F.J. Arnold, Wijchen, The Netherlands: Circular border.
Mr and Mrs Black, Guildford, Surrey: Sunflower border.
Captain and Mrs J.B. Blackett, Arbigland Gardens, Kirkland, Dumfries and Galloway, Scotland: Acid border.
Sir Kenneth MP and Lady Carlisle, Wyken Hall, Bury St Edmunds, Suffolk: Evergreen, Herb borders.
Mr and Mrs Carter, Rowden Gardens, Brentnor, Devon: Giant plants border.
Mrs Beth Chatto, Colchester, Essex: Dry sun, Damp shade borders.
Mrs Jill Cowley, Chelmsford, Essex: Tulip border.
Mr and Mrs Ivan Dickings, Bedfield, Suffolk: Red, Island, Half-hardy borders.
Mrs Helen Dillon, Ranelagh, Dublin, Eire: Yellow border.
Mr Dennis Fairweather: Harleston, Norfolk: Mobile border.
Mrs Natalie Finch, Colchester, Essex: Rose border.
Lt Col. and Mrs Macleod Matthews, Chenies Manor House, Rickmansworth, Hertfordshire: White border.
Oehme and Van Sweden, California: Grass borders.
Packwood House, Warwickshire: Formal border.
RHS Wisley, Surrey: Autumn border.
Derek St Romaine, Chessington, Surrey: Vegetable border.
Ms Barbara Segall: Sudbury, Suffolk: Clay, Children's borders.
Mr Ernie Taylor, Great Barr, Birmingham: Annual border.
Mrs Maureen Thompson, Long Melford, Suffolk: Vertical, Contained, Foliage, Romantic borders.
Ms Julie Toll, Stevenage, Hertfordshire: Sand border at Chelsea Garden Show.
Lady Tollemache, Helmingham Hall, Stowmarket, Suffolk: Summer border.
Mr David Way, Southover, Maidstone, Kent: Damp sun, Meditation, Cottage, Penstemon borders.